PAMPERED COWBOY

A Guide to Western Theme B&Bs, Hotels, Ranches, and Resorts in Texas

Johnny D. Boggs

Republic of Texas Press

Library of Congress Cataloging-in-Publication Data

Boggs, Johnny D.
  Pampered cowboy: a guide to western theme B&Bs, hotels, ranches,
  and resorts in Texas / Johnny D. Boggs.
        p.   cm.
  Includes bibliographical references and index.
  ISBN 1-55622-782-5 (pbk.)
  1. Bed and breakfast accommodations—Texas—Guidebooks.
  2. Hotels—Texas—Guidebooks. I. Title.

  TX907.3.T4 B64   2000
  647.94764'03--dc21   00-035299
                                                  CIP

© 2000, Johnny D. Boggs

All Rights Reserved

Printed in the United States of America

Photos by author except where otherwise noted.

ISBN 1-55622-782-5
10 9 8 7 6 5 4 3 2 1
0004

All inquiries for volume purchases of this book should be addressed to
Wordware Publishing, Inc., at 2320 Los Rios Boulevard, Plano, Texas 75074.
Telephone inquiries may be made by calling:

(972) 423-0090

For Mary Louise Rawls and Sally Gladwin

Contents

Contents

Acknowledgements

First, I could never have written this book without the hospitality and kindness of the various innkeepers, hosts, owners, and staff who took the time to show me around and answer my questions. But I also owe a great deal of gratitude and thanks to the following:

San Miguel Photo Lab of Las Vegas, New Mexico, provided the bulk of my photo developing and enlargements. For the photographers among you, my photos were shot exclusively using Pentax SLR 35mm cameras with primarily Ilford and Agfa black-and-white print film.

Over the course of three trips that totaled about one month, my 1991 Nissan Pathfinder traversed much of Texas, logging almost 7,000 miles to bring its total mileage to 236,740.6. No flats, no problems, and I only got pulled over once. (A friendly Cleburne officer wondered why I had expired Texas inspection and license stickers but New Mexico plates. I explained to him that I had moved to New Mexico and hadn't scraped the stickers off my windshield, and he let me go. Those stickers came off, by the way, as soon as I got home.)

Jeff and Lisa Rogers of Dallas provided a handy way station, complete with a much-appreciated washing machine and dryer and a comfortable sofa and bed that I used between research stops at B&Bs, hotels, ranches, and resorts.

William E. Butterworth IV of *Boys' Life* magazine tipped me off to Rough Creek Lodge; Mike Blakely pointed me to the Y.O. Ranch Resort Hotel and Conference Center. I am also grateful to Bed & Breakfast Texas-Style and the Texas Hotel & Motel Association for their help.

Acknowledgements

Finally, I must thank my wife, Lisa Smith, who is still speaking to me despite the fact that I visited these great spots in Texas while leaving her alone with one high-maintenance, low-intelligence basset hound.

Introduction

Just about everybody, at one time or another, wanted to grow up to be a cowboy or cowgirl. Shoot, since the days of the half-dime novels, cowboys have been romanticized and glorified. That love affair continued with Owen Wister's *The Virginian* and on through the fiction of Zane Grey, Luke Short, Ernest Haycox, Max Brand, Louis L'Amour... with movies starring William S. Hart, Harry Carey, John Wayne, Gary Cooper, Randolph Scott, Joel McCrea... with television shows such as *Rawhide, Gunsmoke, Bonanza, The Virginian, High Chaparral....* The list goes on.

Think Texas, and the images that come to mind often include longhorns and cowboys. Texas has never forgotten its heritage. Just consider the names of the National Football League, National Basketball Association, and Major League Baseball franchises in Dallas-Fort Worth: Cowboys, Mavericks, Rangers.

The truth of the matter, though, is the life of a cowboy in the late nineteenth century was far from romantic and glorious. Cowboys made about a dollar a day, worked from sunup to sunset in the broiling sun and biting cold, and seldom, if ever, fought it out with Indians and outlaws, rescued women on runaway stagecoaches, or faced down a gent with a black hat and blacker attitude on some dusty main street. They were far too busy branding calves, shoeing horses, or mending fences. Heck, they couldn't afford all that gunpowder and lead to shoot it out with the baddies.

But the myth persists. And why not? It makes a great story.

Another common mistake is that we speak of cowboys in the past tense. They're out there today, working just as hard, putting hamburgers on our buns and T-bones beside our Texas toast.

They aren't confined to dude ranches and corny shoot-em-ups in tourist towns; they're earning their keep on working cattle ranches.

Western movies aren't as prolific as they used to be; you'll be hard-pressed to find a Western series on TV, and the shelf space for Western novels seems to be shrinking at many bookstores. But the image, myth, and popularity of the cowboy haven't died, especially in Texas, the state that gave birth to the trail drives to Kansas. Cowboys and the Western lifestyle bring more tourist dollars than a ten-gallon Stetson can hold for one simple reason:

We still want to be a cowboy or cowgirl when we grow up.

But we really don't want to rough it for too long.

And in Texas, you don't have to rough it. You can ride a horse up a mountainside and enjoy a good meal and comfortable bed at night. Personally, I like to rough it. I've helped drive cattle until my eyeglasses were hopelessly scratched and my face was wind-burned and blackened by dirt. I've been pitched off a horse a time or two. I've baked in the saddle and shivered in a bedroll. I've strained cowboy coffee with my teeth. These indelible memories come in handy when I'm writing a Western novel or short story.

But I also enjoy a gourmet meal and a soft bed. I like to gaze at stars and soak up history. A handmade pair of Paul Bond boots, a custom Rand's hat, a pair of 501 Levis, and a Stubbs shirt suit me just fine (and set me back financially). I'll admit it: I like to be pampered.

That's what brought me to write this book.

As the title suggests, this is a travel guide to the best Western-theme bed and breakfasts, hotels, ranches, and resorts in Texas. Western-theme, let me explain, can be loosely defined. It's rather obvious that a dude ranch has a Western theme, but hotels, B&Bs, and resorts can be difficult to quantify. Simply put, for the purpose of this book, the Western theme refers to a place's history, location, or décor.

West Texas has long been associated with cowboy culture; South Texas, especially the Hill Country, is known for its myriad dude ranches; and parts of North Texas saw the long herds of cattle moving to the railroads in Kansas. There are plenty of ranches and cowboys in East Texas and other regions, too, but for tourists and cowboy wannabes, I think West Texas, North Texas, and South Texas/Hill Country offer the most diversity.

Also included are sections on cowboy shopping, "I See By Your Outfit . . . ," and cowboy eating, "Ridin' the Chuck Line," because cowboys and cowboy wannabes like to dress the part and enjoy a good meal. You'll also find profiles, "Top Hands," on some of the best in the business who go out of their way to help you. That's the cowboy way.

Enough of this. We're burnin' daylight. It's time to saddle up.

See you on the trail.

B&Bs

B&B at the Ranch

Fort Worth

A bedroom community seems an unlikely spot for a historic bed and breakfast. In fact, I wasn't sure I was on the right road when I turned into The Ranch and drove past modern homes, but the sign at the end of the narrow paved road welcomed me.

Welcome to B&B at the Ranch

Maybe that's why the brochure calls this ranch house that sits on fifteen acres north of Fort Worth "A country place close to the city."

The B&B is about ten minutes from Fort Worth's historic Stockyards district and ten miles from Texas Motor Speedway. If you're driving north from downtown Fort Worth on Main Street (Business 287), look for the Dairy Queen on the left past Saginaw. You'll take the next right past the Dairy Queen on East Bailey Boswell Road. Cross the railroad tracks, round a curve, and take the left fork on Wagley Robertson. About a quarter-mile later, turn left at the first driveway and head on to the Ranch.

Yep, that's close to the city.

Of course, it wasn't always this way.

The Ranch: The Past

Major K.M. Van Zandt, who had commanded the Seventh Texas Infantry at Chickamauga during the Civil War, owned a farming and ranching operation north of Fort Worth. Born in 1836, he became one of the civic leaders of Fort Worth, paying $200 for the lot for the First Christian Church, fighting for a school system, donating the property where the downtown library now stands, and helping start the first railroad in town. You cross the railroad tracks, which run parallel to Highway 287, on the way to the Ranch.

Van Zandt built a mansion on Seventh Street in town (the house burned in 1962) and a summer cottage house on his ranch, which operated from the mid-1800s to the early to middle part of the 1900s. The original house today was a granary on the farm headquarters. The cottage was made of stone, with stone walls surrounding the property.

The oldest part of the house today, the Cattle Baron's Quarters, is said to have originally been a shack that housed some of Van Zandt's slaves. The granary was later converted into a bunkhouse of sorts and served ranch hands until around 1949.

Van Zandt, who had three wives and fourteen children, died in 1930. His grandson, Bill Sloan, moved into the house in 1956 and built an addition in 1962. Sloan used material from the burned mansion, including hand-carved doors and wooden rafters, when he added on to the ranch house.

About twenty-five years ago, the Stewart family bought the ranch. Hosts Scott and Cheryl Stewart turned the historic ranch into a bed and breakfast, opening for business in March 1997.

The Ranch: The Present

B&B at the Ranch is a combination dude ranch (only without the dudes and horses) and bed and breakfast. You'll find tennis courts and a three-hole putting green on the property, and you can pitch horseshoes under the pecan trees. In the main house, originally built in the early 1900s, the living area features a stone fireplace, and there's an antique upright grand piano if you feel like tapping out a tune. A sunroom comes complete with hot tub and plenty of space. The kitchen is modern and huge. Outside you'll also find a party barn that's great for weddings and special parties.

The dining room has 1840s period furniture. On weekends, expect a full country breakfast. A continental breakfast is served weekdays.

Each bedroom features Western decor. The Cattle Baron's Quarters ($149), the most popular room, has a king-size bed and oak rafters. A private patio, surrounded by a stone fence, has an outdoor fireplace, while the sprawling bathroom features a mural by Judy Sager and whirlpool bath.

A hard-to-find staircase leads the way to the appropriately named Hideaway ($159), the only room on the second floor. This is the pseudo-honeymoon suite. Double doors offer a patio view of the rolling plains of North Texas, and the claw-footed bathtub, which can hold 100 gallons, is an original owned by Van Zandt. Check out the massive armoire while you're there. To get the piece of furniture inside, the roof was lifted off the house and a crane lowered the armoire inside.

The Lazy B Ranch Room ($95) and the Wrangler Room ($115) also feature private baths and king-size beds. If you're after privacy, the Smokehouse Cottage ($159) is rustic and authentic. The Smokehouse was originally built for food storage in the 1800s. A screened-in porch offers willow rocking chairs for relaxing. The rooms might be small, but there's a king-sized bed, and the bathroom features a Jacuzzi.

The Cattle Baron's Quarters at B&B at the Ranch is highlighted by the giant bath-room and mural.

B&B at the Ranch isn't the most authentic accommodation you'll find in Texas. But it's completely cowboy, has more than its share of Texas history, and, as the brochure intones, is a touch of country close to the city.

Cowboy Savvy

Don't think just because the Ranch is located off the beaten path that you can't find the amenities of in-town B&Bs. The staff will be happy to make restaurant reservations, and special services such as massages, limousines, and trail rides are also available.

B&B at the Ranch at a Glance

Address: 8275 Wagley Robertson Road, Fort Worth, TX 76131

Phone: (817) 232-5522, (888) 593-0352

Fax: (817) 847-7420

E-mail: bbranch@flash.net

Internet: bandbattheranch.com

Location: One mile north of Saginaw off Business 287 (North Main in Fort Worth) off East Bailey Boswell Road.

Accommodations: Five.

Dining: Breakfast, full on weekends, continental on weekdays.

Rates: weekday $75 to $95, weekend $95 to $159 double occupancy.

Credit cards: All.

Handicap access: Yes.

Smoking: No.

Pets: No.

Things to do: Party barn, piano, six-to-eight-person spa, three-hole putting green, tennis courts.

Season: Open all year.

Casas de Amigos
Bandera

Contrary to popular belief, there is more to Bandera County than simply a plethora of dude ranches. Our case in point today is the small but cozy Casas de Amigos, an adobe residence that looks like it belongs in New Mexico.

Maybe that's because the owners and hosts, J. Pat and Cindy Breedlove, used to run a publishing venture out of Albuquerque.

Casas de Amigos are two guesthouses, or casitas, in the secluded woods off Lower Mason Creek Road. In fact, the Breedloves are neighbors to another often overlooked Bandera B&B, Comanche Creek.

Casas de Amigos: The Past

Casas de Amigos may look like an old hacienda, but it's new. The home is designed after San Miguel de Allende, Mexico. Innovative Concrete Construction Inc. of San Antonio handled the exterior construction, which features walls ten inches thick and a flat-top roof that Cindy Breedlove says you can park a truck on. Of course, you'll have a lot of trouble getting a pickup up those winding wrought iron staircases.

The courtyard area, separating the casitas from the Breedloves's main house, includes a fountain and waterfall, walkways, and plenty of flowers. There are outside patios perfect for a summer cocktail. Two full RV hookups were installed for guests on long trips.

The Breedloves opened their state-of-the-art B&B in the late 1990s.

Casas de Amigos: The Present

Both roomy casitas are filled with original art, and the Breedloves should know a thing or two about art. In New Mexico,

Casas de Amigos offers a little taste of New Mexico in the Texas Hill Country.

they published full-color guides to artists for more than thirty states.

Each guesthouse has one bedroom and a bathroom, plus a living room and full kitchen. One favorite pastime is watching the sunset from the sturdy roof while sipping a margarita. The roof is also a good spot for wildlife viewing.

Since this is a B&B, the rates include breakfast. But this is a special place, so you'll also get a gourmet dinner. Breakfast comes with juice, coffee, fruit, and homemade jellies and jams, and selections range from a New Mexico breakfast burrito to New Orleans French toast to omelets or a country breakfast of biscuits, gravy, and potatoes.

Dinner includes salads, vegetables, bread, dessert, and complimentary beverages. Selections include grilled steaks, barbecue, chicken Kiev, pastas, seafood, and Santa Fe-style Mexican fare. You can dine privately in your casita, on the rooftop, or in the main house.

Oh, one more note about the dining: The meals are the same for all guests, so the first request is what you eat. Get there early.

Cowboy Savvy

In addition to running a B&B, the Breedloves also offer trips deep into Mexico from Bandera through their Adventures Inc. outfit. Rates include bus travel, lodging, snacks, and beverages, and the Breedloves have more than fifteen years experience in group travel. A nine-day, eight-night trip to Mexico's Colonial cities includes stops in San Miguel de Allende, Guanajuato, Zacatecas, and Saltillo. For information, write to Adventures Inc., 446 Live Oak Ridge, Bandera, TX 78003, or call (830) 460-7479.

Casas de Amigos at a Glance

Address: 446 Live Oak Ridge, Bandera, TX 78003
Phone: (830) 460-7479
Fax: (830) 796-3026

E-mail: N/A

Internet: N/A

Location: 2½ miles north of Bandera on Live Oak Ridge off
Lower Mason Creek Road.

Accommodations: 2 guesthouses.

Dining: Breakfast, dinner.

Rates: $79 double occupancy.

Credit cards: None.

Handicap access: No.

Smoking: No.

Pets: No.

Things to do: Massage, horseback riding (off premises),
birding, wildlife viewing. Wine, flowers, event tickets,
additional services.

Season: Open all year.

Comanche Creek
Bed and Breakfast

Bandera

The stone and frame houses sitting on these shaded hills outside of town are cowboy for sure. Between the Western
adornments inside and the frontier architecture outside, visitors
might swear they have been transported back in time to the
1880s.

Course, that satellite dish is a dead giveaway that you're still
in modern times.

Located on slightly less than sixteen acres, Comanche Creek
Bed and Breakfast includes three houses and a pair of hosts in

9

cowboy hats, Viola and Darrell Allen, who could serve as extras on a Western movie. Which might be why Viola Allen landed a part in *All the Pretty Horses*.

Comanche Creek B&B: The Past

The Main House was originally a two-room stone house with a loft built on Mason Creek in the 1870s by either Jerome Strickland or his son, Lewis. The ceiling is eleven feet high, and the original walls are twenty-one inches thick. The highlight of the living room is a giant stone fireplace, on which Jerome Strickland wrote: "Jerome Strickland visited here from California in 1941. I was born here in 1888-April 29." The house has been added on to over the years, including a modern kitchen.

Behind the house sits the Bunk House, said to have been used by a Pony Express outfit (no, not the original Pony Express, which did not run through Texas and went out of business in 1861 with the completion of the cross-country telegraph) in Fredericksburg. The tall shack is more than 120 years old.

Finally, there's the Guest House, which is filled with Victorian decor but has a front porch, complete with rocking chairs and wagon wheels, that makes it look Western on the outside.

Darrell Allen, a carpenter, helped turn the buildings into an original B&B, and Comanche Creek opened in the late 1990s.

Comanche Creek B&B: The Present

Renting the Main House requires advance notice. Usually, a great cowboy breakfast is served in the dining room with plenty of coffee and homemade biscuits. The home is filled with cowboy and Native American decorations, and sitting on the front porch, sipping a cold one with Darrell and Viola, is a fine way to spend the evening.

The Bunk House includes two double beds, central heating and air conditioning, and a private bath. The cypress woodwork was taken from a bar in Bandera that was about to be torn down.

Commanche Creek Bed & Breakfast features several historic structures moved to Bandera.

(It sure is handy to have a carpenter like Darrell on the premises; Darrell and Viola live in the so-called John Wayne House on the property.)

Inside the Guest House, you'll find a double bed, private bath, and central heating and air conditioning. And that antique piece of furniture that looks like a desk? It's actually a roll-out single bed.

Comanche Creek B&B is a delightful Western experience, and Viola Allen wants to add some teepees for those who prefer roughing it to give the property even more of a Western flavor.

Cowboy Savvy

In addition to a hearty breakfast, Viola Allen offers her guests a parting gift: homemade salsa. You can tell her how fiery or mild you like your hot sauce, and when you pack up to leave, she'll be there to wave goodbye and issue the farewell Roy Rogers and Dale Evans made famous: "Happy Trails!"

Comanche Creek B&B at a Glance

Address: 1954 Lower Mason Creek Road, Bandera, TX 78003

Phone: (830) 460-4705

Fax: N/A

E-mail: N/A

Internet: N/A

Location: 2 miles north of Bandera on Lower Mason Creek Road off Highway 173 (2 miles on Lower Mason Creek Road to black wrought iron gate on the right).

Accommodations: Guest House with double bed, antique roll-out single, central heat and air, and bath. Bunk House with 2 double beds, central heat and air, bath. Main House (with advance notice).

Dining: Breakfast included. Dinner available with advance notice.

Rates: $125 daily.

Credit cards: Visa.

Handicap access: No.

Smoking: On porches only.

Pets: No.

Things to do: Nearby shopping, horseback riding, golf, fishing, hiking.

Season: Open year round.

Elizabeth Crockett B&B

Granbury

Don't expect to find a coonskin cap and flintlock rifle here. Elizabeth Crockett didn't move to Texas from Tennessee until 1853, seventeen years after husband Davy died at the Alamo. Elizabeth Crockett never lived in this house, but her granddaughter did, and owners Jennifer and Rick Nichols named this Queen Anne style house after Colonel Davy's second bride.

The B&B is a labor of love for the Nicholses, who bought the house in 1988 while they were working for TU Electric at the Comanche Peak Steam Electric Station. It took years to renovate and opened in 1996 as an upscale bed and breakfast filled with period furniture, Victorian antiques, and—oh, yes—two cats.

Elizabeth Crockett B&B: The Past

The house, a state historic landmark, is known as the Thrash-Landers-Hiner house, named after the first three owners. Granbury's first mayor, P.H. Thrash, had the home built in 1880. Saloon owner George Landers became the second owner before J.J. Hiner, a lawyer, district attorney, and president of the City National Bank bought the place. Hiner then sold the house to his brother, Thomas, who happened to be married to Olivia

Elvira Crockett, the youngest granddaughter of David and Elizabeth.

If you're interested, Elizabeth Crockett came to Texas when she was sixty-five, having been granted more than 4,000 acres in present-day Hood County. She moved south with her son Robert and daughters Elvira and Mathilda. They first settled in Ellis County, then near the town of Granbury. Robert built a log cabin in 1856 on 1,200 acres, then built another cabin two years later about a half mile away. Elizabeth lived in that cabin until she died on January 31, 1860, at the age of seventy-two. In the 1880s Robert moved to Granbury.

Elizabeth Crockett B&B: The Present

Soft music greets guests when they enter the parlor. Feel free to roam the house, from the library, dining and game rooms to the garden out back, and check out those wood shingles. Twelve-foot ceilings and oak woodwork stand out, and Oriental rugs cover hardwood floors. All of the four guestrooms, which have private baths, are located upstairs.

The Miss Mollie Room includes a Renaissance Revival double bed. Many guests call this the "blue" room because of the blue damask wall covering. The Miss Rose Room has a queen-size bed and a floral wall covering. The bathroom includes an original claw-foot tub, while a window offers a view of the backyard. The Miss Margaret Room, known as the "grandmother room," has a queen-size bed with a hand-crocheted coverlet, and the added bathroom includes an antique toilet.

The Miss Olivia room, named after Crockett's granddaughter, took the longest to renovate (with the exception of the master bedroom, which usually isn't available for rental) because of extensive termite damage (no worry today, though). This room also has a queen-size bed and a good view of the Hood County Courthouse.

Elizabeth Crockett B&B was once the home of Davy and Elizabeth Crockett's youngest granddaughter.

Don't forget, like most upscale B&Bs, young children are not permitted. And also remember that the two cats have run of the house, but that doesn't mean they have any business in your bedroom.

Cowboy Savvy

Elizabeth Crockett's gravesite is located six miles east of Granbury off U.S. Highway 377 and F.M. Road 167 at Acton State Historical Park, the smallest state park in Texas. The monument went up in 1911. The park is for day use only. For information, call (817) 645-4215.

Elizabeth Crockett B&B at a Glance

Address: 201 W. Pearl St., Granbury, TX 76048

Phone: (817) 573-7208

Fax: (817) 573-7209

E-mail: crockettb&b@itexas.net
Internet: www2.itexas.net/~crockettb&b
Location: One block west of the square in historical downtown.
Accommodations: Four.
Dining: Breakfast.
Rates: $93 to $98.
Credit cards: American Express, Discover, MasterCard, Visa.
Handicap access: No.
Smoking: No.
Pets: No.
Things to do: Walking distance to shopping, dining, and live
    entertainment.
Season: Open all year.

Etta's Place

Fort Worth

It's highly unlikely that Etta Place, back when she was hanging out with a couple of likable outlaws known as Butch Cassidy and the Sundance Kid, ever fared this well: spacious rooms with massages, 24-hour dry cleaning, and horse-drawn carriage rides (okay, maybe she had the latter frequently), and a breakfast of white wine sauce and sausages, eggs Florentine with rosemary potatoes, or perhaps a scrambled-eggs pizza.

Etta's Place in downtown Fort Worth is the perfect hideaway named after an outlaw queen. Each of the ten rooms is named after a member of Cassidy's Hole in the Wall Gang or a female pal. The outside of the building is designed to re-create the original building put up at this location in the 1800s.

This isn't a historical structure by any means. Yet it is full of Texas history.

Etta's Place: The Past

The first building at this location went up in the 1880s and over the years housed everything from a dry goods store to a car showroom to an appliance store. Edward P. Bass's Caravan of Dreams opened next door in 1983 and began staging jazz concerts and other artists from country to blues and folk to rock. The four-level complex includes a theater and reception facilities. In 1990 Caravan of Dreams took over the building at 200 West Third Street to house traveling entertainers performing at Caravan of Dreams.

In November 1996 Etta's Place (still owned by Caravan of Dreams) opened as a bed and breakfast inn for the sophisticated traveler or honeymooner. The idea was to blend an elegant B&B with a high-rise hotel.

It seems to have worked. Etta's Place is popular with tourists, corporate travelers, and couples needing a place for a wedding reception or even a small wedding (up to 125 guests).

Etta's Place: The Present

Rooms vary in size from 300 square feet to the 700-square-foot suites (basically, the suites were efficiency apartments). Each room has its own private bath, and the suites include full kitchens. A coffee nook on the third floor is stocked with, yes, coffee. Five rooms have queen-size beds ($125), all furnished in Texas antiques.

Laura's Lounge ($145) has two adjoining rooms, king-sized bed, and an ice machine and overlooks Sundance Square. Oh, since each room is named after a Hole in the Wall member or his female friend, just who was Laura? Well, Laura Bullion was a farm gal from Knickerbocker, Texas, the story goes, but she took the name of Della Rose and became known as the "Rose of the

Wild Bunch." She married outlaw Will Carver, but after Will met his demise in a shootout in 1907, she took up with Ben Kilpatrick.

Etta Place has a claim to Fort Worth, too, although she remains pretty much a mystery to historians. One story says she was a Fort Worth schoolteacher until she was wooed by Harry Longabaugh, better known as the Sundance Kid (for those of you keeping score, Butch Cassidy's real name was Robert Leroy Parker). Legend has it that Etta traveled with Butch and Sundance to South America in 1901 but came back to the United States five or six years later. Butch and Sundance were killed in Bolivia in 1911, or maybe they weren't. Etta is said to have returned to teaching in Denver... or maybe it was Oregon... or it could have been Cowtown. One story says Etta, going by the name Eunice Gray, died in a fire in a Fort Worth boardinghouse in 1962.

Back to the rooms. For names, there are Annie's Suite (named after Annie Rogers, who fell in love with Kid Curry), Ben's Bedroom (Ben Kilpatrick, who died in a 1912 train robbery), Will's Refuge (Will Carver, Laura Bullion's beau who wound up on the losing end of a gunfight), Lillie's Pad (Lillie Davis, a Palestine girl who went to work in Fannie Porter's Fort Worth brothel), Maude's Parlor (Maude Walker, another of Fannie's girls), Etta's Attic, Sundance's Suite, and Butch's Hideout.

The suites ($150) have king-size beds, seating areas, white-tile kitchenettes. A split-level loft ($165) is the perfect honeymoon escape with a wooden spiral staircase leading to a queen-size iron bed in the loft. Downstairs, you'll find a seating area, dining room, and bachelor's kitchen.

Breakfast is served (7-9 A.M. weekdays, 9-11 A.M. weekends) in the dining room or in the atrium patio. Other common areas include the library, the music room (complete with Steinway piano), and a circular stairway that heads up to the coffee nook and playroom.

The parlor showcases Etta's Place as an elegant B&B retreat in downtown Fort Worth.

Etta's Place caters to the corporate traveler, with computer modem access, fax, and copier machines. Previous guests at Etta's Place might take note that a new phone system is scheduled to go on line in 2000. The previous system was routed through Caravan of Dreams, which didn't always seem to work so well.

It's easier to get a room on weekdays, but you'll need to book well in advance for weekends. That's because there is no down time at Etta's Place (although January and August can be slow).

Etta's Place is a unique downtown B&B that blends Texas chic with a little bit of history, even if Butch Cassidy never stayed here.

Cowboy Savvy

So, where do you park? Etta's Place has no parking, but the inn is flanked by three parking lots. The B&B can validate parking at one of those lots. Compared to downtown Dallas, parking in downtown Cowtown usually isn't at such a premium. Meters on the street are free after 6 P.M. and on weekends, and a quarter can buy you 50 minutes at some meters.

Etta's Place at a Glance

Address: 200 W. Third St., Fort Worth, TX 76102

Phone: (817) 654-0267

Fax: (817) 878-2560

E-mail: etta@flash.net

Internet: www.caravanofdreams.com

Location: Downtown, in historic Sundance Square district.

Accommodations: Ten.

Dining: Breakfast.

Rates: $125 to $165.

Credit cards: All.

Handicap access: Yes.

Smoking: No.

Pets: No.

Things to do: Swedish massage, meeting and reception facilities, catering, wedding receptions. Adjacent to Caravan of Dreams, Rooftop Grotto Bar and walking distance to dining, entertainment, and shopping.

Season: Open all year.

Fort McKavett Guest House

Fort McKavett

Charles and Lill Kothmann have never stayed in a bed and breakfast, yet here they are, third-generation ranchers running a guesthouse when not tending to the livestock grazing on their 1,260 acres.

Oh, on top of those chores, Charles is a U.S. Department of Agriculture "field man."

So what made them turn this storehouse into a guesthouse just down the road from the ruins of an old frontier army post?

"It's hard, hard, hard to make a living in agriculture these days," Charles says.

Adds Lill: "It was a way to supplement our income. There has been a lot of visitors to Fort McKavett State Historical Park wanting a place to stay. This gives people a place to get away from the city."

It seems like a wise investment.

General William T. Sherman once called Fort McKavett the prettiest post in Texas, and this rugged country on the Edwards Plateau adjoining the Hill Country in the Concho Valley hasn't changed much over the past century. But the state park doesn't even allow camping, and the nearest lodgings can be found in Junction on Interstate 10. So if you stay there, you're missing some of the darkest, clearest skies in Texas, perfect for stargazing.

Fort McKavett Guest House: The Past

"My great-grandfather came to Fort McKavett the second time it was established, and had a saloon and a contract to furnish hay and grain to the army," Lill Kothmann says. "That was a pretty good income."

21

Born in Germany in 1836, William Lehne moved to Fredericksburg, Texas, in 1852, and married another German immigrant, Theresa Jung. They moved to Fort McKavett in 1868.

Fort McKavett had originally been established in 1852 on a high bluff on the San Saba River, but it was abandoned seven years later. Confederate troops occupied the garrison during the Civil War, and the Federal army reoccupied the fort in 1868. Colonel Ranald S. Mackenzie ordered the fort rebuilt, and a parasite community, called Scabtown, sprang up nearby.

William Lehne died in 1877, leaving behind six children and his widow. One of his sons, Ed, born in 1874, married Lillie Arnold around 1916, and they settled on this ranch. Now the Kothmanns run the ranch, opening the guesthouse in 1998.

Fort McKavett Guest House: The Present

If you don't like your breakfast when you stay here, blame yourself. You're on your own. You cook it yourself. A menu is provided upon arrival, and after choosing what you want, the food is delivered to the guesthouse. I opted for bacon, eggs, and homemade biscuits. Imagine my surprise at the amount of food when I was delivered two big eggs, six slices of bacon, and seven biscuits ready for cooking. Don't fear cooking the biscuits; they came with instructions. A small bottle of orange juice and a can of coffee were also included.

If you're staying for more than a night, you might want to pick up some cooking supplies since restaurants, like hotels, are scarce in this neck of the woods.

And let's not forget the cookies and snacks waiting for me when I checked in. I regret not trying the coffee cake.

The guesthouse, located just behind the Kothmanns' residence, has two bedrooms, a bath, full kitchen, and living area. Outside you'll find a large porch, picnic table, and grill. The house can sleep up to six people, perfect for families.

Fort McKavett Guest House gives visitors a glimpse of life on a working ranch.

Feeling active? Well, hiking and biking trails lead over the ranch, passing several Indian middens (don't call 'em mounds). You'll pass several varieties of cactus and oak. "In the spring, if it rains, we have very nice wildflowers," Lill says.

If you're interested in wildlife viewing, foxes (gray and red), deer, porcupines, and armadillos are common. Easier to spot, however, are the livestock. The Kothmanns raise cattle, goats, and sheep for market. The cattle are Brangus, an Angus-Brahma cross. Rambouillet ewes and black-faced Suffolk rams are sheared for their wool in May, and the goats are raised as a meat herd. A few horses can been seen and photographed, also.

Perhaps the Kothmanns will invite you when they feed the goats and sheep. "This is a big hit with the kids and adults, too," Lill says.

Feel free to venture out on your own. But remember these rules:

- Leave gates as you find them. Nothing irritates a rancher more than having someone leave a gate open.
- Don't approach or feed any animals—including the cows, horses, goats, and sheep.
- Don't pick flowers or plants or remove artifacts.
- Hunting and shooting (guns or archery) are prohibited.

But you don't have to go exploring. The Guest House is full of plenty of reading material, and the beds are comfortable. Besides, at how many B&Bs can you look out the kitchen window while brewing coffee and stare at a horse and a cow?

FYI: Credit cards aren't accepted here. You can pay by cash, personal check, traveler's check, or money order.

Fort McKavett Guest House is special, and the Kothmanns know all about Texas hospitality. So what if they've never stayed in a B&B? They could teach a lot of innkeepers a thing or two.

Cowboy Savvy

Fort McKavett State Historical Park isn't the best preserved fort in Texas, but it's certainly photogenic. The ruins have often been compared to crumbling Scottish castles. The fort features a fine museum. In addition to famed Indian campaigner Ranald Mackenzie, the fort was home to the black Buffalo Soldiers. Sergeant Emanuel Stance, with the Ninth Cavalry's F Troop, won the Medal of Honor for his bravery in action against Apaches in 1870 while stationed at the fort.

The park is open daily, except Christmas Day, from 8 A.M. to 5 P.M. It features an interpretive nature trail, gift shop, picnic sites, and occasional reenactments.

Of course, there's another way to see the area, and that's getting a special tour with Pete Crothers at the nearby Fort Trading Post. Crothers might best be described as "an independent guy," and the Trading Post is a unique country store/dance hall/place where you can drink a cold beer and enjoy the country. Crothers also has a replica 1929 Model A Roadster. You haven't toured this part of the country until you've ridden with Pete.

Fort McKavett Guest House at a Glance

Address: HC 87, Box 208, Fort McKavett, TX 76841-9703

Phone: (915) 396-2949

Fax: N/A

E-mail: lillyth@airmail.net

Internet: www.webwalkers.com/b&b

Location: Six miles south of Fort McKavett on State Highway 1674, about 20 miles north of Interstate 10.

Accommodations: Separate Guest House sleeps six, has two bedrooms, one bath, complete kitchen, grill, picnic table, living area, large porch for sittin' and rockin'.

Dining: Snacks and coffee cake furnished on arrival. Breakfast on your own from menu selections.

Rates: $80 per night double occupancy ($15 for each person extra over 2 years old). $375 for six nights double occupancy ($40 per day for each additional guest).

Credit cards: None.

Handicap access: Yes.

Smoking: No.

Pets: No.

Things to do: Birding, stargazing, wildlife and domestic livestock viewing, marked trails for hiking or viewing which pass Indian middens and native plants. Fort McKavett State Historical Park is nearby.

Season: Open all year.

Hotel Turkey

Turkey

Welcome to the hometown of the late Bob Wills, the king of Western Swing music, who still plays a major influence on country-western music (and if you don't believe me, ask Merle Haggard or members of Asleep at the Wheel). This small Panhandle town, which, naturally, houses the Bob Wills Museum and a Bob Wills monument, sits on the way to the rugged and beautiful Caprock Canyons State Park.

Turkey is also home of Hotel Turkey, a fifteen-room bed-and-breakfast inn run by Gary and Suzie Johnson that is listed on the state and national historic registries.

Hotel Turkey is a treasure, earning recognition from *Texas Highways*, *Texas Monthly*, The Associated Press, and even David Letterman. As Gary Johnson quotes from one write-up: It has stood "the test of time."

Hotel Turkey: The Past

The two-story brick building cost $50,000 to build in 1927, and unlike other frontier hotels, Hotel Turkey has never closed its doors for overnight guests. The hotel has had a few owners over those years, but it remained under the ownership of one family for approximately fifty years.

Scott and Jane Johnson bought the hotel in the late 1980s and turned it into a B&B operation. Up until then, Hotel Turkey had been a hotel. The Johnsons ran the business until selling out to Scott's cousin, Gary, and wife, Suzie, in 1996.

Explains Gary: "We had been court reporters for twenty-something years in Arkansas and looking for a change, and Turkey is my hometown, and my mom still lived here, and even though I had been gone from Turkey for thirty-seven years and never dreamed of—quote—coming back home, it's just one of those things that happened, and it was just natural. My cousin and his wife had some other irons in the fire and were looking for some help and so here we are."

Hotel Turkey: The Present

And here the guests keep on coming. About 75 percent of the visitors come to get away and enjoy Turkey's relaxed pace. The fifteen rooms (thirteen on the second story) are filled with period antiques, resulting in a 1920s decor. Rooms have neither telephones nor televisions. Seven rooms have private baths, four rooms have shared bathrooms, and the bathrooms for the remaining four rooms are located down the hall.

"When you walk in our front door it's kind of like going back in time seventy years," Gary Johnson says. "The hotel is full of antiques, and it sometimes has been touted or referred to as a living museum, which means: Yeah, we've got a bunch of old stuff here but you use it. It's not just there to look at. You sleep on it and you eat on it and you sit on it and do whatever."

A country breakfast is always a treat. Sweet-potato pancakes are a staple at Hotel Turkey, served with sausage, eggs, juice, coffee, sometimes blueberry muffins, and occasionally biscuits and gravy. Of course, on Thanksgiving Day, a turkey dinner is also served. After all, a Thanksgiving turkey dinner at Hotel Turkey in Turkey, Texas, sounds natural, doesn't it?

In their four years as owners of Hotel Turkey, the Johnsons have yet to discover a peak season. Hunters and families often come in the winter, Caprock Canyons is always a lure, and the hotel is great for seminars, business meetings, and weddings. It also attracts a lot of class and family reunions, as well as church retreats.

"If I were going to be a visitor to the Turkey, Texas, area, knowing about the weather conditions, I would probably try to come in April or May or possibly September-October," Gary Johnson says. "I think those months are probably more suited for outdoor activity without extreme hot and extreme cold, even though, yes, we can get some hot weather in September and we can get some cold weather in April, but generally speaking it's pretty pleasant that time of year."

Now a historic bed-and-breakfast, Hotel Turkey has been open since it was first built in 1927.

Cowboy Savvy

But you can't spend the night at Hotel Turkey during the Bob Wills Day celebration. The hotel is reserved for the Wills family and the Texas Playboys. Bob Wills Day is the last Saturday in April and draws some 15,000 fans to the town of 500. It's a pilgrimage for many Wills aficionados to come to Turkey every year. In fact, some show up ten days to two weeks before Bob Wills Day for Western Swing jam sessions and camaraderie.

Visitors are still invited to drop in at Hotel Turkey to look at the downstairs area and maybe chat with the Johnsons.

"We like for people to do that because that makes them want to come back so they can see the rest of the hotel and maybe come back and stay with us another time," Gary Johnson says, "but, no, we are not open for reservations during that week or weekend, and I could rent 4,000 rooms if I had them."

Hotel Turkey at a Glance

Address: P.O. Box 37, Turkey, TX 79261

Phone: (806) 423-1151, (800) 657-7110

Fax: N/A

E-mail: suziej@caprock-spur.com

Internet: www.turkeytexas.com

Location: Third and Alexander, one block north of Main Street. Turn by grocery store.

Accommodations: 15, 13 upstairs; 7 with private baths, 4 with shared baths, 4 with baths at end of hall; dining room seats 36.

Dining: Breakfast only unless with group of 15 or more.

Rates: $75-$100.

Credit cards: American Express, MasterCard, Visa.

Handicap access: Yes (one room with bath on first floor).

Smoking: No.

Pets: No.

Things to do: Tennis courts and nice patio area on site. Caprock Canyons State Park 15 miles west. Bob Wills Museum nearby.

Huckaby House B&B

Jacksboro

On the windswept Southern plains, Jacksboro looks like something out of a Larry McMurtry novel. This is petroleum and ranching country, with a few antique shops, a lot of history, and several downtown buildings made of native limestone. Maybe that's what makes the Huckaby House stand out.

This charming Victorian house sits far off Highway 380 less than two blocks from the downtown intersection at Highway 199. It wasn't always that way. In 1969 Leon Hawkins bought the house and had it moved to the back of the lot.

Bill and Judy Wolfe bought the house in 1997 and quickly turned it into a bed and breakfast, filling the house with antiques and giving it a Texas flavor from the blueberry French toast or cheese blintzes for breakfast to the shingle of the original owner that hangs in the hall.

Huckaby House B&B: The Past

Doctor F.G. Huckabay (the Wolfes changed the spelling to lessen confusion on pronunciation) and his wife, Ida, built this house in 1902. "He was an old country doctor who made his rounds in his buggy," Bill Wolfe says, "and was one of the original pioneer doctors in the county."

Ida Lasater Huckabay is probably most famous for her history, *Ninety-Four Years in Jack County, 1854-1948*, first published in 1949. A first edition of that book, by the way, can fetch more than $400.

In 1969 Hawkins, a former undertaker, and his wife, Ruth, bought the property. In addition to moving the house off the street, they also added some rooms to the original structure.

Then came the Wolfes, who moved back to Texas from Colorado. They found the house was up for sale and decided to make the B&B plunge, adding two bathrooms and opening for business in October 1997, only three months after buying the historic home. The B&B also serves as home for the Wolfes, who both have full-time jobs but enjoy their hospitality gig.

Huckaby House B&B: The Present

All four bedrooms are upstairs, and there are two sitting areas as well. Each room features canopy beds, family memorabilia, and is named after an early Jack County settlement.

Cottontail Thicket, done in pink and white, has a toy box, which is popular with guests who bring their small children with them. "It's one of our grandkids' favorite rooms because it's got the toys in it," Wolfe says.

"I think there was only one original bedroom upstairs when the Huckabays had it," Wolfe says. "Because it has two outside windows with gables on it, and that's the only room upstairs with windows."

Los Valley, done in white, is what Judy Wolfe considers the bridal or honeymoon suite and is probably the most popular room. "It has a real warm, inviting feel to it," Bill Wolfe says, "and a very comfortable bed, and I think most people really enjoy that room."

The Squaw Mountain room, named after the community where Judy grew up, is done in green and includes an old sewing machine and an old rocking chair. An antique bedspread covers the bed. The final room, Wizard Wells, is done in a deep burgundy. With a deer head, this room has more of a masculine feel to it, Wolfe notes.

Squaw Mountain and Cottontail Thicket share a large bathroom. The other two rooms have private baths.

A gourmet breakfast is served "wherever our guests would like," Wolfe says. The patio is popular in spring and fall, and breakfast in bed is available on request, but usually the meals are taken downstairs in the dining room.

Phones aren't in the rooms, but there is phone access. That's because the Huckaby House is designed as a getaway for people who want a little peace and quiet.

The Huckaby House in historic Jacksboro was once the home of a frontier Texas doctor.

Cowboy Savvy

Fort Richardson, now a state historic park with camping facilities, historic buildings, and a museum, played an important part in Texas settlement as an active military post from 1866 to 1878. And the town of Jacksboro was the site of one of the most historic—and often overlooked—Western trials.

In 1871 a band of Kiowa Indians including Satanta, Satank, and Big Tree led an attack on a wagon train, killing seven men, and escaped to Fort Sill in present-day Oklahoma. After being captured by the army, the chiefs were brought back to Jacksboro to stand trial. Ever the warrior, Satank freed himself, wounded a guard, and was shot to death shortly after the party left Fort Sill.

The Jacksboro trial was the first attempt to subject Indians to white law, although, with a jury of cowboys and ranchers unlikely to look at Indians with impartiality, it was anything but just. To no one's surprise, Satanta and Big Tree were found guilty after a three-day trial and sentenced to hang. After a plea by the governor, who feared a bloody Indian war if the two were hanged, the sentence was commuted to life in prison. The two Kiowas were later paroled and returned to the reservation, but after another uprising, Satanta was returned to Huntsville prison where he committed suicide in 1878.

Huckaby House B&B at a Glance

Address: 333 W. Belknap, Jacksboro, TX 76458

Phone: (940) 567-6222

Fax: (940) 567-5343

E-mail: N/A

Internet: N/A

Location: 1½ blocks west of downtown on Highway 380 (Belknap), across from bakery.

Accommodations: Four.

Dining: Breakfast.

Rates: $100 to $150 double occupancy.

Credit cards: MasterCard, Visa.

Handicap access: No.

Smoking: No.

Pets: No (some exceptions).

Things to do: Bird and deer watching from back deck. Nearby Fort Richardson State Historic Park offers an interpretive center, historic buildings, and hiking trails.

Season: Open all year.

Mariposa Ranch Bed & Breakfast

Brenham

About halfway between Brenham and Somerville, on F.M. 390 just off Highway 36 North, sits not your ordinary farmhouse.

Make that houses.

Johnna and Charles "Doc" Chamberlain have moved several historic buildings onto their small, 98-acre ranch. They didn't actually intend to go into the B&B business—Doc, a retired vascular surgeon, still sees a few patients here—but soon discovered that the houses, especially after Johnna's decorating, were perfect B&Bs.

Guests come to get away from the city, where they can marvel at Doc's collection of antique maps hanging in the hallway of the main house, go hiking or biking through the fields, or just sit back and read a good book and take a nap.

Breakfast is first-rate, with conversations between guests accentuated by the classical music playing. Mariposa Ranch blends country peace with Victorian elegance, the perfect romantic getaway and an easy drive from Austin and Houston.

Mariposa Ranch: The Past

Originally called Oakridge, the property was a 500-acre ranch before it was divided up and sold off, and the Chamberlains began their house-moving/saving projects in 1991. A plantation-style house, circa 1870, came from Brenham. Originally L-shaped, the structure has been added on to over the years.

A run-down, overgrown log cabin, originally built around 1825, was about to be bulldozed before the Chamberlains stepped in. The two-story Greek Revival house, built in 1836, was said to have been a doctor's house, and the original homestead from the 1880s was on the property when the Chamberlains moved in.

Other buildings on site include the Fern Oaks Cottage; a bunkhouse where ranch hands used to live; and the office of Doctor Red, a faith-healer from nearby Independence during the 1860s. The office hasn't been restored, and no guest, or ghost for that matter, would want to spend the night there. But maybe someday the Chamberlains will use their magic touch and re-create another masterpiece.

Pretty soon the Chamberlains realized they not only had a home—they live in the main house—but a B&B as well. Mariposa (Spanish for butterfly) Ranch Bed & Breakfast opened in the early 1990s and has earned accolades in *Texas Highways* and *Southern Living* magazines as well as being featured in Washington County Historical Society tours.

Mariposa Ranch: The Present

Shaded by live oaks, the Plantation Home is only missing Scarlett and Rhett sipping mint julep tea and rocking on the front porch while enjoying the sunset. Two rooms are available to rent in the house, which has twelve-foot ceilings and hardwood floors. The Tejas Room has a queen-size bed and a rustic, masculine decor. Its private bathroom has both a claw-foot tub and a separate shower. The Brazos Room comes with one queen and one twin bed, with a claw-foot tub. By the way, now's a good time to point out that Mariposa Ranch accepts "well-behaved" children.

The Texas Ranger Cabin pays tribute to the Texas Rangers— and I don't mean the baseball team. From the porch, you can sometimes see the lights from Bryan and College Station. In addition to Ranger decor, the log cabin includes a giant stone fireplace and wood stove. Downstairs is a queen-size sleeper sofa, while a queen bed is found in the upstairs loft.

Two suites are located in the Greek Revival home, named the Independence House. Jennifer's Suite has a king-size canopy bed and two twin beds, and Kathleen's Suite comes with a queen-size and a double bed. Both suites have fireplaces and old-fashioned soaking tubs.

The restored original farmhouse is the Reinauer Guest House, a three-bedroom, two-bath home with a large living room and full kitchen. It's the perfect place for family reunions, complete with one queen and three double beds.

Fern Oaks Cottage, with porch, fireplace, and queen bed, is known as the "honeymoon suite," and the Ranch Hand's bunkhouse is equipped with two twin beds and a queen-size sleeper sofa.

Mariposa Ranch can also be rented out for weddings and parties. By the way, it is a ranch, with cattle, other livestock, and a slew of dogs. If you decide to go for a walk or bike ride, feel free to explore the property. Just remember the Number One Ranch Rule:

Close all gates!

Mariposa Ranch's circa-1870 Plantation Home was moved from Brenham in the early 1990s.

Cowboy Savvy

Brenham and nearby towns Burton, Chappell Hill, Independence, and Washington are full of Texas history. In fact, Washington County is known as the "Birthplace of Texas." Any good student of Texas history can tell you that the Republic of Texas was born at Washington-on-the-Brazos when Texans declared their independence from Mexico on March 2, 1836. Washington-on-the-Brazos State Historical Park and the Star of the Republic Museum are located in Washington, but the entire county is full of other historic sites.

A Washington County Historical Markers Guide is available at Mariposa Ranch, you can check out the Brenham Heritage Museum, or feel free to explore on your own.

Mariposa Ranch Bed & Breakfast at a Glance

Address: 8904 Mariposa Lane, Brenham, TX 77833

Phone: (409) 836-4737

Fax: (409) 836-4712

E-mail: mariposainn@earthlink.net

Internet: www.mariposaranch.com

Location: One-half mile east of Highway 36 between Brenham and Somerville off F.M. 390 (La Bahia Road).

Accommodations: 9 rooms with private baths.

Dining: Breakfast.

Rates: $90-$155 double occupancy.

Credit cards: MasterCard, Visa.

Handicap access: No.

Smoking: No.

Pets: No.

Things to do: Shopping, hiking, fishing, lake, historic sites nearby.

Season: Open all year.

Miss Molly's Hotel

Fort Worth

The upstairs joint at 109 1/2 West Exchange Avenue has gone from one extreme to the other, from boardinghouse to cathouse to bed and breakfast. Miss Molly's opened as a B&B in 1989, making it the oldest commercial bed and breakfast in Fort Worth.

Miss Molly's has seven rooms restored in the manner of the original boardinghouse. Those seven rooms, homey and comfy, share three bathrooms (two with old-style tubs) down the hall. Sam Colt may have made all men equal in the Old West with his six-shooter, owner Mark Hancock points out, but at Miss Molly's the bathrobes are the great equalizers. The eighth room, a suite (and the old madam's quarters), has Victorian decor and a private bath.

If the real estate adage "location, location, location" is true, then this two-story brick building is prime. Located in Cowtown's historic stockyards, Miss Molly's is upstairs from the Star Cafe, just across the street from the famous M.L. Leddy's Western outfitter and walking (or crawling) distance from famous North Fort Worth watering holes Billy Bob's and the White Elephant Saloon.

The Tarantula Train runs from Grapevine to the Stockyards, and there are plenty of other shopping ventures and restaurants. Street events include Pioneer Days in September and the Chisholm Trail Roundup in June.

Of course, the Stockyards area wasn't always so hospitable and tourist-friendly.

Miss Molly's: The Past

The upstairs has always been some type of lodging ever since the building went up in 1910. Amelia Ellsner was a "straight-laced" woman who ran the Palace Rooms boardinghouse from

1924 into the 1930s. Miss Amelia was so prim and proper that she would demand proof of marriage before renting out one of her rooms to a couple. The next proprietress, however, had no such morals.

Miss Josie served as the madam at the Gayette Hotel (the letters can be faintly spotted on the back of the building) from the 1940s until the middle 1960s. She dealt with a shadier business. You'd find gambling going on sometimes, but the big business was prostitution.

Later occupants included a "black-market" dentist (when the Stockyards catered to a rough clientele) and the Stockyards Fine Arts Colony (when the upstairs digs became more reputable). In the late 1980s, when Billy Bob's went into bankruptcy, the artists moved out. When Billy Bob's came back and the Stockyards district began to revitalize, Mark Hancock decided to turn the upstairs quarters into a B&B.

Billy Bob's, the Stockyards, and Miss Molly's have been going strong ever since.

Miss Molly's: The Present

The key to any B&B is great service, and Miss Molly's staff is about as friendly as you'll find. Mark and Alice Hancock have gone out of their way to re-create an inn with a turn-of-the-century feel and a few modern conveniences. Innkeeper Kelly Jones continues that tradition.

Each room has a theme related to the history of Fort Worth and Texas, while two are named after the landladies of the building. Miss Josie's is the Victorian suite, while Miss Amelia's has a white iron double bed, lace curtains, and hand-worked linens.

The Cowboy's room has a bunkhouse flavor, complete with twin iron beds and a potbelly stove. Saddles, spurs, and chaps complete the flavor and re-create the Cowtown's cowboy history. Long before Billy Bob's opened, Fort Worth served as a stop for waddies driving longhorns from South Texas up the Chisholm Trail to the Kansas railheads.

The Cattlemen's room is a tribute to the cowboys' boss and the men who made the Stockyards famous for buying and selling beef. This room comes complete with a double bed of carved oak with mounted longhorns and a matching dresser.

Fort Worth was the site of the world's first indoor rodeo, and the Fort Worth Livestock and Stock Show Rodeo, which started in 1896, remains a Cowtown tradition, although the site has moved from the Stockyards to the larger Will Rogers Memorial Coliseum in the arts district. Miss Molly's Rodeo room has a double iron bed, pictures, posters, and other rodeo decor.

Cowtown never was an oil town, but the Oilmen room celebrates the movers and shakers of the heyday of the Texas oil fields. The iron double bed and oak chifforobe dresser and wash stand re-create the image of the oilmen from Spindletop, Borger, and other Texas sites.

The railroad arrived in the summer of 1876, so the Railroader pays homage to this aspect of Cowtown. There's an ivory double iron bed, along with an oak dresser and steamer trunk.

Last but not least, the Gunslinger room has a double bed and is surrounded by photographs of gunfighters, the good, the bad, and the ugly. Fort Worth was the site of one of the last great gunfights in the West, when Luke Short laid T.I. "Longhaired Jim" Courtright in his grave, and the famous photograph of Butch Cassidy and the Wild Bunch was taken in Fort Worth. The Gunslinger has lavender walls. Lavender? For a gunslinger? Well, John Wayne wore a lot of pink shirts in his movies, so I guess that's appropriate.

The furniture isn't museum quality, but the pieces come from North Texas and re-create the image of a boardinghouse from the early 1900s.

Breakfast is generally served buffet-style, usually in the parlor underneath the stained glass skylight. And don't be scared off

Miss Molly's Hotel re-creates an early 1900s boardinghouse for visitors to Fort Worth's Stockyards.

by those three shared bathrooms. They're spacious, and the bathrobes hanging on the doors of the rooms are of good quality. You can buy one, too, if you like, for $60.

Cowboy Savvy

Parking can be at a premium in the Stockyards, but Miss Molly's offers a parking pass that is sent when you make your reservations or can be handed out once you arrive. The B&B also sends out a "Howdy" letter that explains policies and other pertinent information. And although Miss Molly's doesn't allow pets, Mark Hancock is quick to point out that "the livery is down the street."

Miss Molly's Hotel at a Glance

Address: 109 1/2 W. Exchange Ave., Fort Worth, TX 76106-8508

Phone: (800) 996-6559, (817) 626-1522

Fax: (817) 625-2723

E-mail: missmollys@travelbase.com

Internet: www.missmollys.com

Location: 2.5 miles north of downtown Fort Worth in Stockyards National Historic District.

Accommodations: Eight.

Dining: Breakfast, buffet-style.

Rates: $80 to $200.

Credit cards: All.

Handicap access: No.

Smoking: No.

Pets: No.

Things to do: Walking distance to shopping, restaurants, and honky-tonks.

Season: Open all year.

Ragtime Ranch Inn

Elgin

It can be hard to find upscale bed-and-breakfasts that allow children. And pets? Forget it.

Yet both are welcome at this heavily shaded gem hidden in the country surrounding Elgin, 23 miles east of Austin.

The Ragtime Ranch Inn promotes "the good country life," and it's definitely country. To get here, you travel 3.2 miles down Second Street (F.M. Road 3000) from downtown Elgin to the dirt County Road 96 (which is easily missed). After another 1.3 bumpy miles, you turn left—by now there are signs showing the way to the Inn—on County Road 98, which dumps onto the property of Roberta Butler and Debbie Jameson a half mile later.

How pet friendly is the Inn?

"We found we love pets more than kids," Roberta says with a smile.

Adds Debbie: "If you're going to take a dog on vacation with you, it has to be a well-behaved animal."

The Inn includes two 12-by-12-foot stalls with 12-by-40-foot runs, plus two private pastures. The only requirement is that you bring your own feed and keep it in the tack room separating the stalls. There are stacks of dog towels, too, because the hosts have learned that dogs are dogs, and that little fishing pond on the property is always inviting for a pooch, even a city canine.

But don't think that children won't have a good time here either—and they are also quite welcome.

Besides, there are dogs, donkeys, and chickens—I told you this was the country—and Roberta and Debbie enjoy having children help them gather the eggs. And the donkeys? They like being petted.

Ragtime Ranch Inn: The Past

Roberta Butler was born and raised in Jacksonville, Florida, and Debbie Jameson is a Houston native. They moved to Elgin in the late 1980s and built the Inn next to their home in 1995.

Why?

"We had friends who came to visit," Debbie answers, "and they wouldn't leave so we decided to make them pay."

That's a pretty solid reason.

"Our biggest claim is that I've stayed in 4,000 hotels, and Roberta has stayed in about 3,000," Debbie adds, "so we know what we didn't like."

Such as: "Why on earth do you have to put clothes on to find ice?" Debbie asks. Roberta says: "Why should I have to lean over backward to take a shower? And what's with those little bars of soap to shower with?"

Well, you'll find an icemaker in the refrigerator in your guestroom at the Inn, the soap is Texas-sized bath bars, and the showerheads were installed by a 6-foot-4 builder who made his mark to place the shower head by reaching up. Unless you're being recruited by every Division I college in the country as a center and the National Basketball Association wants you to play today, you probably won't have to wrench your back trying to lather up your hair in the shower.

Ragtime Ranch Inn: The Present

"We're it," Roberta says. "There are no employees."

The Ragtime Ranch Inn features four rooms. They are basically 450-square-foot efficiency apartments, each with a large bathroom (and that shower head is really up there), fireplace, two queen-size beds, microwave, coffeepot, television, and refrigerator. Plates, glasses, mugs, bowls, and utensils are provided for your continental breakfast. The rooms don't have telephones, but you'll find one in the office, along with a fax machine and reading and video library.

Three rooms have screened-in porches, and the third offers a private deck. A ranch-style porch wraps around the Inn, and there are rocking chairs and plenty of Roberta's handmade wreaths (feel free to place an order for one). Each room also has its own Christmas tree from the day after Thanksgiving until the New Year.

When you check in you pick out your complimentary breakfast, which is put in a basket in the refrigerator for you to prepare at your leisure. "We'd rather have cocktails with our guests when they check in rather than try to get to know them in the morning," Roberta says. "That way, they don't have to see us in the morning unless they really want to."

Breakfast includes two full pots of coffee, regular and decaffeinated. Yup, that was another one of Roberta's and Debbie's pet peeves about today's hotels. Each guest also has a choice of any two of the following juices per person: orange, grapefruit, apple, or V-8. To eat, you choose two of these: croissant, English muffin, blueberry muffin, bacon breakfast taco, ham breakfast taco, sausage breakfast taco, chorizo and egg breakfast taco, carne guisada wrap, or Meyer's Elgin sausage wrap. The tacos and wraps are locally made.

"You did know that Elgin is the sausage capital of Texas?" Roberta asks.

Yeah, sure, absolutely. Who doesn't know that?

For lunch or dinner, Elgin has a fine selection of restaurants—including a lot of barbecue and sausage—and there's a picnic area at the Inn complete with barbecue grills for guests who feel like working for their grub.

Sitting on 37 acres, the Inn has plenty of trails for hikers, offering ample bird watching opportunities. During the spring and summer, wildflowers are abundant (U.S. Highway 290, which runs through Elgin, is known as the Bluebonnet Parkway). There are butterfly gardens and that stocked fishing pond that dogs

The Ragtime Ranch Inn features a wrap-around porch in the shaded country near Elgin.

love. Fishing is allowed, and you can keep your catch if you promise to eat it.

The Inn also handles weddings and reunions—"We enjoy the cooking part," Roberta says, "because we're here anyway." Drive-by guests are not allowed, so call first.

Of course, you'd have to know where you are going to find this place. As I have mentioned, this is the country.

And that's what attracts most of the Inn's guests.

"Most of our business is people out of the city who want to get to the country," Roberta says. "If they're going back home, we give them some eggs to take with them."

Cowboy Savvy

Elgin's historic downtown district includes many specialty shops, and the town also includes many antique shops. In fact, U.S. 290 could be called the Antique Highway for its myriad antique stores between Elgin and Brenham. Depending on the shop, you can find furniture, china, crystal, books, magazines, photographs, firearms, clothes . . . just about everything. In addition to its "Bluebonnet" nickname as well as being part of the Texas Independence Trail, the highway is also called the "Presidential Corridor" because it connects the presidential libraries of Lyndon B. Johnson in Austin and George Bush in College Station.

Ragtime Ranch Inn at a Glance

Address: 203 Ragtime Ranch Road, P.O. Box 575, Elgin, TX
        78621
Phone: (800) 800-9743, (512) 285-9599
Fax: (512) 285-9651
E-mail: ragtimeinn@earthlink.net
Internet: www.ragtimeinn.com
Accommodations: 4 rooms with private baths and entrance.
        Every room has 2 queen beds, fireplace, refrigerator with

icemaker, microwave, coffeemaker, and kitchenware; 3 rooms have screened porches; 1 has a private deck.

Dining: Continental in-room breakfast included. Separate catering menu available.

Rates: $95 single or double occupancy. $10 each additional person.

Credit cards: American Express, Discover, MasterCard, Visa.

Handicap access: Limited.

Smoking: Yes.

Pets: Yes.

Things to do: Gift shop on premises. Swimming pool. Stocked fishing pond, picnic/party area with barbecue grills. Birding. Hiking. Donkeys on premises.

Season: Open all year.

The Rosemary Mansion on Main Street

Waxahachie

About 27 miles south of Dallas, Waxahachie has become a popular getaway for antique shopping and its collection of gingerbread Victorian-style houses. Film crews have become enamored with the turn-of-the-century architecture (commercial and residential). Among the movies shot here include *Bonnie and Clyde*, *Tender Mercies*, and *Places in the Heart*.

One of the most splendid locations is the Rosemary Mansion on Main Street, which Dennis and Judy Cross opened as a B&B in 1997. The mansion isn't named after the friendly cat roaming the grounds (the Crosses will put her away if the house is full or if you're allergic); it's named after the herb, "the symbol of friendship and remembrance."

That's fitting because you'll find a lot of herbs, grown in the gardens outside, used in your breakfast, and chances are you'll always remember the friendly innkeepers and the luxurious accommodations.

"We always planned to open this as a B&B," Dennis Cross says, "and we wanted to do an upscale B&B, something a little different. I tell newcomers who haven't been to a B&B before to act like they're visiting Grandma's house."

Hmmmmm. The way I remember things, Grandma lived in a dark trailer filled with snuff cans. But then, Grandma never married P.A. Chapman.

Rosemary Mansion: The Past

P.A. Chapman was an oilman, rancher, and banker, definitely a "wheeler-dealer," Cross points out. He owned a ranch in South Texas and served as a front man for an oil and gas deal as a banker while taking a quarter interest as a silent partner in the oil company. The deal netted $40 million; Chapman's cut was a cool $10 million.

That ain't bad jack now, but imagine World War I dollars.

Or consider the story about how Chapman bought his ranch in South Texas. The story goes—Chapman relatives say it's true—Chapman learned that Captain Richard King of the famous King Ranch was interested in selling some 76,000 acres (at a dollar an acre) in South Texas. When Chapman found out that Captain King was on a train leaving Houston, he got on the train and managed to sit beside King.

The two men struck up a conversation and got to know each other as the train lumbered across Texas. Chapman soon let it drop that he was interested in buying some ranch land, and King said, well, he happened to have some land for sale.

Chapman: "I'm interested in buying it."

King: "Son, that's $76,000 cash."

Chapman reached under his seat, pulled up his carpetbag and replied, "It just so happens that I have $76,000 on me."

They closed the deal on the train.

True story? I don't know, but it sure is a great one.

Never fond of the city, Chapman decided to build a "Sunday house" on the cotton fields outside of Waxahachie. It's hard to imagine that this home sat on open prairie some eighty years ago. Today, it's on Main Street and surrounded by houses.

In 1916 Chapman hired Dallas architect C.W. Bulger to build his home and gave him free reign. The result was a Georgian Revival mansion that some people thought was overly extravagant. After all, this house had two-and-a-half baths plus a full bath for servants and another bathroom in the guesthouse. A four-and-a-half-bath estate isn't to be taken lightly these days, so imagine what it was like in 1916.

Chapman and Bulger opted to wire the house for electricity (another extravagance) and filled the mansion with chandeliers (three are originals today) and beautiful furnishings. And since they were showing off, they imported Philippine mahogany some 12,000 miles for the inside. That cost a dollar a board foot back then. "And today," Cross adds with a chuckle, "Philippine mahogany still costs about a dollar a board foot."

The house was used primarily for board of director meetings and the extended family. It's funny, Cross notes, how the wealthy acted in the early twentieth century. Cousins would marry cousins, simply to keep the wealth in the family.

Chapman's daughter took over the house after he died and lived there until the 1950s when the mansion was bought by banker Oliver Clift. Oddly enough, Clift had delivered ice to the workers when they were building the house in 1916 and told them he would own that house someday. Clift sold the house to a Dallas doctor in the 1970s, and the Crosses took over in the mid-1990s.

The hardwood floors, woodwork, and even much of the glass are original. The only major changes have been the addition of two bathrooms, the remodeling of the kitchen area, and the upgrading of the heating, cooling, electricity, and plumbing. The carriage house, however, has undergone some alterations over time.

Rosemary Mansion: The Present

The Rosemary Mansion sits on an acre covered with gardens, fountains, and walkways. A conservatory, which is entered through a bell tower, is ideal for small weddings and other events. The Crosses have filled the mansion with antiques and original art, most of the paintings of landscapes and outdoor scenes. The collection is, in Dennis Cross's word, "eclectic." "We're not big on paintings of people," he says, although he points out that the portrait of George Armstrong Custer hangs on the wall "because we liked the painting."

The front hall, the most formal part of the house, is filled with French antiques. A sea captain's map chest and a 1920 chandelier are found in the dining room. The bedrooms include the Victorian Rose Room, Edwardian Violet Room, Country Scented-Geranium Suite, French Lavender Bridal Suite, and the Garden's View Guesthouse (which has two guestrooms and a butler's kitchen). All of the rooms and suites have private baths and are decorated with period antiques and herbal-flower decor. Quality B&Bs and hotels often include mouthwash, shampoos, and various toiletries, but the Rosemary is the only place I've found where there is shaving cream in the bathroom.

We might as well point out that because of the antiques and elegance, the Rosemary Mansion isn't really suited for children. Of course, would you want to bring your kids along on a romantic getaway?

Breakfast is served downstairs in the dining room, on china and crystal. It's served in courses, too, so don't leave after the fruit. Judy Cross laughs while telling the story of one couple who came downstairs, sipped the gourmet coffee, and ate the fruit. "Dennis came into the kitchen and said, 'I think they've left,'" she recalls. "He went upstairs, knocked on the door, and asked if they were feeling all right. They said they were, they just thought that was the breakfast."

Not hardly.

As Dennis Cross points out, "No one has ever left here hungry."

When you check in, your room and house keys are attached on a silver spoon. That symbolizes the "silver-spoon" treatment that Dennis and Judy Cross aim to give their guests.

The Rosemary Mansion on Main Street was once the home of a Texas "wheeler-dealer" banker and rancher.

"There's a movement to go too casual and not use old things," Dennis Cross says. "We just like to go the other direction and have a feeling of elegance."

Cowboy Savvy

Waxahachie has changed a lot from the rough town that sprang up along the old Shawnee Trail. Driving maps are available to lead visitors on a journey past the wonderful commercial and residential architecture, from shotgun houses to Neoclassical Revival style. The circa-1902 Chautauqua Building, where Will Rogers and John Philip Sousa performed, is among the last standing today, and the circa-1895 Ellis County Courthouse, made of red sandstone and granite, is one of the most photographed courthouses in the state.

For the record, Waxahachie is an old Indian word meaning "Cow buffalo standing in the creek."

The Rosemary Mansion On Main Street at a Glance

Address: 903 W. Main St., Waxahachie, TX 75165

Phone: (972) 935-9439, (972) 923-1181

Fax: (972) 923-1199

E-mail: denwcross@aol.com

Internet: www.texasguides.com/rosemarymansion.html
    and www.hat.org

Location: East on Business 287 off Interstate I-35E, exit 401B.

Accommodations: Five.

Dining: Breakfast, evening hors d'oeuvres.

Rates: $100 to $250 double occupancy (extra for extra guests).

Credit cards: All.

Handicap access: No.

Smoking: In arbor only.

Pets: No.

Things to do: Gardens, fountains, and conservatory on grounds. Angelica Conservatory can hold weddings and special parties.

Season: Open all year.

Texas Stagecoach Inn

Vanderpool

The clear, peaceful Sabinal River gently rolls past the ancient maple trees that tower over the cedars and oaks in one of the prettiest places in Texas. Three acres of riverfront property would be a dream for any photographer (or landscape artist for that matter), but the picturesque white frame mansion sitting just off Highway 187 is an added bonus.

And that's just on the outside.

Inside, the Texas Stagecoach Inn—which never was a stage stop, by the way—is a charming bed and breakfast inn, with exceptional hosts (David Camp is a landscape artist, and wife Karen is a knockout cook).

The Camps are continuing a tradition that Bob Thompson started more than a century ago.

Texas Stagecoach Inn: The Past

Back in 1885 Bob Thompson and his family were the first whites to settle in Sabinal Canyon. They built a prominent two-story home on a pier and beam foundation.

Thompson, who came from Arkansas, had eighteen children, nine with his first wife and nine more with his second. Feeding that many mouths must have been quite a chore on the Texas frontier, but the Thompsons didn't stop there.

"They were known for their hospitality," Karen Camp says. "They hailed in travelers at mealtimes to sit at the table."

After the home burned in 1918, it was rebuilt on the same pier and beam foundation. In the 1960s the new owner expanded the house to the south, north, and west.

The house had always been a private home, and it still is. The Camps live here (with children Lindsay and Trevor), but when they bought the property, Karen says, "we had a vision to create a bed and breakfast. We thought this area needed more upscale accommodations for the discriminating visitors."

The Texas Stagecoach Inn opened in 1994.

Texas Stagecoach Inn: The Present

Each guestroom and suite is named after a geographic point in the region.

Although the private bathroom is definitely 1960s, the decor in the downstairs Thompson Peak Room, named after—you guessed it—Bob Thompson, is true West, from the queen-size "Heart of Texas" bed with its beautiful log-cabin quilt to plenty of Texana reading material.

More Old West furniture, most of it from the WR Dallas line, and another queen-size "Heart of Texas" bed can be found in the downstairs Panther Hill Room. The story goes that on the hill south of the inn, Bob Thompson was attacked by a panther while horseback riding. Thompson killed the panther with his knife, although his horse died in the attack.

The downstairs suite is the Cottonwood Canyon Suite, the proverbial "honeymoon suite," with a king-size bed. Upstairs, the Button Willow Canyon Suite features two double beds, one king-size bed, and access to the balcony. The latter suite is perfect for families, and the inn accepts children ages ten and up.

"The two canyons are on private property," Karen says, "but can be seen from the upstairs balcony. They're said to be two of the most beautiful and long forgotten canyons in the area."

All rooms and suites have private baths. You won't find any telephones or televisions, but there is plenty of reading material, from books (mostly Texana) to magazines.

Oh, and let's not forget David Camp. His paintings decorate many of the walls in the inn. Prices are available on request.

Paddles and canoes are located on the banks of the river behind the house. Guests who take to the Sabinal should stay on the inn's property (from white fence to white fence). Fishing is allowed—catch-and-release only—but swimming is prohibited.

Coffee is ready by 7:30 A.M. Breakfast will be found on the buffet in Aunt Dottie's kitchen at 8:30 A.M. The food, such as the pumpkin pancakes with praline sauce, is wonderful. You might not want to leave.

There are three peak seasons at the Inn. The spring brings bird watchers, the summer attracts tourists interested in the various nature activities, and the fall is known for a glorious display of colorful foliage on the maples so red, yellow, and orange that you'd swear you were in New England. Of course, winter isn't a bad time to visit the Vanderpool area either.

So, how did the Camps come up with the name Texas Stagecoach Inn?

"The house was remodeled to look like an early stagecoach inn with a New Orleans flavor," Karen Camp says. "Although the house was never a stage stop, since it looks so much like one, we felt it was very appropriate."

The Texas Stagecoach Inn never served as an actual stage stop but had a reputation for hospitality.

Cowboy Savvy

Vanderpool's major tourist destination is Lost Maples State Natural Area, a 2,174.2-acre park in Bandera and Real Counties that draws some 200,000 visitors each year.

Most of them come for the fall foliage, usually at its peak from mid-October to mid-November, highlighted by a large stand of rare Uvalde bigtooth (or canyon) maples.

Others come for the birds, including the green kingfisher, golden-cheeked warbler, and black-capped vireo. But the park also showcases limestone canyons and has eleven miles of hiking trails, plus campsites, picnic areas, an interpretive center, and gift store.

The park, which opened in 1979, is located five miles north of Vanderpool on Ranch Road 187. The address is HC 01, Box 156, Vanderpool, TX 78885, and the phone number is (830) 966-3413.

Texas Stagecoach Inn at a Glance

Address: HC 02, Box 166, Highway 187, Vanderpool, TX 78885

Phone: (830) 966-6272, (888) 965-6272

Fax: (830) 966-6273 (Call 6272 number first)

E-mail: stageinn@swtexas.net

Internet: www.bbhost.com/txstagecoachinn

Location: South on State Highway 187 between Vanderpool and Utopia.

Accommodations: 4.

Dining: Breakfast served on kitchen buffet, buffet-style.

Rates: $85-$115 double occupancy. Minimum stay of two nights on weekends and three nights on holidays.

Credit cards: None.

Handicap access: No.

Smoking: No.

Pets: No.

Things to do: Canoeing and fishing (catch-and-release only) on property.

Season: Open all year.

The Veranda

Fort Davis

If you didn't know this delightful bed-and-breakfast country inn existed, you would probably never find it. Not that many people turn off Highway 17 onto a dirt road in downtown Fort Davis, unless they want to visit the Overland Trail or Neill Doll Museums.

The Veranda isn't really off the beaten path. It's only a block west of the courthouse, but it is a great getaway. The rooms are huge, the hardwood floors shiny, and the breakfast filling and a treat.

Besides, this B&B is as much a part of Fort Davis's history as any structure in town.

Veranda: The Past

In 1883 county surveyor W.S. Lempert built an E-shaped hotel one block off the San Antonio-El Paso road, "the Interstate 10 of its time," owner-host Kathie Woods says. The Lempert was more than a hotel. Horses could be bought, sold, or exchanged at the stables at the addition, and hacks and buggies were available for rent.

Lempert sold the complex to James Stewart (no, not Jimmy the actor) four years later, and the building became known as the Stewart Hotel. Stewart, in turn, sold out to J.H. Clark in 1927, and the building was turned into the Clark Apartments. Many locals still refer to the building as the Clark Apartments. In 1982 the property was sold again in an attempt to turn it into a hotel. That didn't quite work out, but in 1989 Paul and Kathie Woods took over and began converting the building into a B&B. After several long weekends and a sabbatical (Paul teaches architecture at Texas A&M University), the rechristened Veranda (named after the veranda out front) opened for business in July 1994.

Veranda: The Present

This is a territorial-style frontier hotel—don't call it Victorian—with huge rooms. Since Paul and Kathie Woods run this as a getaway, you won't find telephones or televisions in your room. The adobe walls are nearly two feet thick, with twelve-foot-high ceilings and oak and pine floors. These floors aren't original, by the way. In 1883 the floors would have been made of wide planks that rested on the ground. When indoor plumbing became necessary in the 1920s, the easiest way to hide the pipes was to raise the floors.

The Veranda includes eleven rooms and two guesthouses. All but two rooms have connecting baths; Egyptian cotton velour robes are provided for the suites where the bathrooms are located a few steps down the hall. These bathrooms are not shared.

Three rooms have two queen-size beds, while the eight other suites and rooms have one king-size bed. Most bathrooms have modern tub-showers, but Room 3, with mahogany furnishings and a green marble washstand, features an old-timey soaking tub.

Just behind the main building sits the adobe Carriage House—yes, it was the carriage house in the early days of the Lempert—which includes two bedrooms with king-size beds, a living room, small kitchen, and one bathroom.

The Garden Cottage, once the bathhouse for the hotel, has a queen-size bed and a large tiled shower.

The Veranda took its name from the front porch, perfect for stargazing on clear West Texas nights.

You'll find two courtyards on the grounds, with plenty of shade, even gardens and an orchard.

Wake up hungry, because Kathie Woods serves a delightful breakfast. Coffee is usually ready by 7 A.M., and breakfast can be served at 8 or 9 A.M. Hot biscuits made from scratch, a scrumptious egg souffle, bacon, sausage, juice, and fresh fruit (Fort Davis produces plenty of apples) awaited me on my stay, but feel free to request a lighter meal.

"This building is truly a treasure," Kathie Woods says.

So is staying here.

Cowboy Savvy

Legend has it that in December 1884 the Lempert Hotel played host to an exciting group of guests. Fort Davis historian Barry Scobee wrote that on December 13, Quanah Parker and two other Comanches (Rising Sun and Nan Notes) stayed at the hotel with an Indian agent. They were in the area on a search for peyote on Mitre Peak. Quanah Parker was the son of a Comanche chief and Cynthia Ann Parker, a white woman kidnapped in a raid in 1836. Quanah led the Comanches to war against white encroachment until he was forced to surrender in the 1870s. Afterward, he led his people down the road to peace and became quite a celebrity.

Did he really stay at the Lempert? Scobee didn't cite his sources, newspapers from the period haven't survived, and the original hotel ledgers haven't been located. Fort Davis post records don't mention this visit, nor do any biographies of Quanah, and the Texas State Library points out that peyote really isn't native to Mitre Peak.

But it makes a great story. Besides, maybe the great Comanche did walk these same halls more than a hundred years ago. That puts hotel guests with some pretty good company.

The Veranda at a Glance

Address: P.O. Box 1238, Fort Davis, TX 79734

Phone: (888) 383-2847, (915) 426-2233

Fax: (419) 844-5361

E-mail: info@theveranda.com

Internet: www.theveranda.com

Location: 1 block west of the courthouse in town.

Accommodations: 14.

Dining: Breakfast included.

Rates: $80-$130 double occupancy.

Credit cards: Discover, MasterCard, Visa.

Handicap access: No.

Smoking: No (including porches and grounds).

Pets: No.

Things to do: Walking distance to downtown shopping, stargazing from the porch.

Season: Open all year.

Hotels

Captain Shepard's Inn

(Operated by The Gage Hotel)
Marathon

Albion E. Shepard, a former sea captain who had sailed the Aegean Sea, gave this old Southern Pacific Railroad stop many things, not the least of which has to be the town's name. Captain Shepard said the country reminded him of Marathon, Greece.

With a population of about 600, Marathon, Texas, is a sleepy hamlet that serves as one of the gateways to Big Bend National Park. Most people stop here to gas up (a word of advice if you're coming in on a Sunday morning: You'll likely find the filling stations closed until after church) or make a pit stop.

Actually, Marathon has quite a few things to offer and two outstanding places to hang your hat for a night. The historic Gage Hotel is the most famous, but Captain Shepard's Inn is a hidden treasure just behind the brick and adobe (okay, stucco) hotel on the corner of Avenue D and Second Street.

Don't bother looking for street signs. Turn north off U.S. Highway 90 at the first street on the east side of The Gage. If you're staying at the Inn, you'll need to check in at The Gage first.

"People love this place," says Nelson Vansidener, general manager of The Gage, which leases and operates the Inn owned by Russ Tidwell of Austin. "Many make specific requests for it."

And why not? Like The Gage, Captain Shepard's Inn is filled with Western and Southwestern decor and wonderfully authentic hardwood floors. The two-story Greek Revival house makes a perfect family reunion location or a romantic getaway without the traffic you'll find at The Gage.

"This is the kind of house that is really a home," Vansidener says.

That's what Captain Shepard meant for it to be, too.

Captain Shepard's Inn: The Past

Albion Shepard was hired to help survey the Southern Pacific line from San Antonio, Texas, to Los Angeles, California, in 1881. The following year he got to name the Texas water stops between Del Rio and El Paso. He must have liked Marathon, because not only did he name the Texas water stop, he decided to make it his home, buying land on March 10, 1882.

He formed the Iron Mountain Ranch, where he ran some 25,000 sheep, and began laying out town lots in 1885. With the area supporting a growing population of about 130, Shepard established the first post office in town in 1883 and served as the first postmaster. Around the turn of the century, he began to build his two-story home with a carriage house about a hundred yards from the railroad tracks. The house has been occupied since its completion.

After the Shepard family, the Hess family, who ran a merchant and ranching operation, owned the house. In 1995 restoration of the historic home was completed, and the Inn opened that March.

Captain Shepard's Inn: The Present

The Inn has five spacious bedrooms, each with private baths and porches. Check out the antler chandelier when you enter the Inn. One television and a telephone are located in a common area, and there's a full-size kitchen complete with stove, coffeemaker, and dishwasher. Breakfast, by the way, isn't included in your stay, but there are a few restaurants in town, including the pricey but excellent Cafe Cenizo at The Gage. Because the Inn is operated by The Gage, the hotel facilities, including the swimming pool, are available to guests at Captain Shepard's Inn.

The bedrooms are located in the main house. The only downstairs room ($105) includes a queen-size antique brass bed and a Jacuzzi tub.

The four upstairs bedrooms ($84-$95) have queen, three-quarter, or double beds. Rooms 3 and 4 can be set up as connecting rooms. Room 4, by the way, has a private bath down the hall.

The carriage house, circa 1890, is a two-bedroom, one-bath "bunkhouse," complete with porch, kitchenette, fireplace, and living area. It rents for $120 for the first four people (remember, you're sharing one bathroom), and $15 for each additional person.

It's an easy walk to U.S. Highway 90, Marathon's main drag, for a casual stroll down the boardwalk. Marathon, surprisingly, offers plenty of shopping opportunities. Even more shocking might be just how upscale some of these stores are. You'll find galleries, antiques, and cowboy collectibles, or you might opt for a shake and a burger at Johnny B's, an old-fashioned soda fountain (closed on Wednesdays).

Or you can take a walking or driving tour through town. Check out the brick bank vault on Avenue D near the Inn. It's all that remains after a fire destroyed the Marathon bank in 1920. South of the railroad tracks you'll find the old jail, cemetery, and the Guayule Plant site (not much there other than stones used in the extraction process). Believe it or not, Marathon was once home of the first and only processing plant in the United States that obtained raw natural rubber from the Big Bend-native guayule plant. The factory, built in 1907, shut down in 1926.

Marathon, Vansidener notes, is "really a unique kind of place and very enjoyable. It's nice for a little respite."

Captain Shepard gave Marathon its name before building his home, now run by The Gage Hotel.

Cowboy Savvy

If you elect to stay at Captain Shepard's Inn and cook your own grub, Marathon sports just one grocery store. It's located on the east side of Avenue D near the Inn. Hours are 6:30 A.M.-6:30 P.M. Monday through Saturday and noon to 4 P.M. Sunday. Of course, this is the remote Big Bend region, so you might do better to stock up on the necessities at the nearest big city (which isn't very near).

Captain Shepard's Inn at a Glance

Address: C/O The Gage, P.O. Box 46, Marathon, TX 79842

Phone: (800) 884-4243

Fax: (915) 386-4510

E-mail: welcome@gagehotel.com

Internet: www.gagehotel.com

Location: Behind The Gage Hotel off U.S. Highway 90 in town.

Accommodations: 5 rooms plus two-bedroom, one-bath carriage house.

Dining: N/A.

Rates: Main house $85-$105, carriage house $120 for first four persons, $15 for each additional person.

Credit cards: American Express, Discover, MasterCard, Visa

Handicap access: No.

Smoking: No.

Pets: Yes (small).

Things to do: Walking distance to restaurants and shopping.

Season: Open all year.

The Driskill Hotel

Austin

The elite organization Leading Hotels of the World includes 315 hotels and resorts in 68 countries. You'll find one member in Texas: Austin's fabulous Driskill Hotel.

Meeting the group's tough standards puts the Driskill in company with Paris's Hotel Ritz and London's The Connaught, and once you walk into the Austin landmark's lobby you'll understand how the Driskill made the cut.

The hard part is simply to choose what is the most striking and elegant: The elaborate, hand-laid marble floor, the custom-made stained glass dome, the stunning hand-painted ceiling, the towering floor-to-ceiling columns, or even the turn-of-the-century furniture.

Heck, this place is fit for a president. So it shouldn't come as a surprise that Bill Clinton has stayed here. So has Hillary Rodham Clinton. It was a favorite of Lyndon Johnson, who had his first date with Lady Bird here and found out that he had been elected president in 1964 while waiting for the returns in what is today called the Jim Hogg Parlor, one of many meeting rooms on the mezzanine.

In 2000 the hotel completed a three-year, $35 million restoration, returning the Driskill to its builder's original dream: an exquisite hotel full of Victorian charm.

A portrait of Jesse Lincoln Driskill looks down on the lobby, and you have to think that the one-time Texas cattle baron is mighty pleased.

The Driskill Hotel: The Past

Jesse Driskill was born in Tennessee in 1824 and lived in Missouri for four years before moving to Bastrop, Texas, in the early 1850s. He became a merchant and lived in San Antonio, San Marcos, and Bryan with his wife and family. In 1857 Driskill went into the cattle business and made a fortune supplying the Confederate army with beef. By the end of the war, though, Driskill was broke, but he rebuilt his cattle herds and re-established himself as a cattle king during the early years of the cattle drives to the railheads in Kansas.

In 1871 Driskill moved his family to Austin, and he established other ranches in South Texas, Kansas, and Dakota Territory. In Austin in the mid-1880s, he envisioned a hotel and bought a half block bordered by Brazos, Sixth, and Seventh Streets for $7,500.

The Richardsonian-Romanesque-style hotel was designed by Jasper N. Preston and Sons of Austin. The four-story building (the mezzanine was created in subsequent remodeling), constructed of cream-colored limestone, opened on December 20, 1886. It featured sixty guestrooms and four suites, heated by steam, with many arched entryways and corner balconies, not to mention several dining rooms, including the main sky-lit room, a billiard room, saloon, and barbershop.

It was one of the top hotels in Texas.

But business wasn't all that great, and a few months later Driskill was forced to close the towering hotel because of financial difficulties. Driskill sold the hotel two years later, and the building began a long series of more sales and new owners. One owner made part of the lobby a bank—the vault today houses the hotel's safe-deposit boxes. The guestrooms were remodeled in 1923, and a fifteen-story tower was added in 1929. Yet the hotel continued to change hands and was even threatened with closure in the early 1970s.

Today the Driskill, which is also a member of the National Trust Historic Hotels of America, is privately owned and managed by the same group that operates the Chatham Bars Inn of Chatham, Massachusetts; The Cincinnatian of Cincinnati, Ohio; and Le Pavillion of New Orleans, Louisiana.

And Jesse Driskill?

Legend has it that Driskill's fortune was wiped out during the savage winter that struck the Northern Plains in 1888 and that the one-time cattle baron never recovered from his losses. He suffered a stroke and died on May 3, 1890.

The Driskill Hotel: The Present

Today, the Driskill has 190 guestrooms and 15 suites. The rooms in the original building feature ceilings nineteen feet high, stunning crown molding, and opulent bathrooms with Brazilian marble tile. In the Tower, you'll find narrower hallways and a lighter decor. "We think the rooms here have more of a bed-and-breakfast feel," says Tracy Fitz, the hotel's executive assistant manager. Tower guestrooms are painted in traditional Hill Country colors, while the bathrooms have more of an Art Deco look to them with black-and-white tile floors. The Art Deco look was intentional, Fitz notes. Remember the Tower was completed in 1929. "We tried to keep the decor true to the building," Fitz says.

All of the rooms and suites have a nineteenth-century feel to them, complete with wrought-iron beds and custom furnishings, but come with twenty-first-century amenities.

Rooms include a telephone in the bathroom, on the desk, and on the nightstand, voice message service, and high-speed computer lines. A digital alarm clock, bathrobes, and hair dryer are provided, along with magazines, cable television, weekday newspapers, and a private safe-deposit box in the room. The Driskill also provides 24-hour room and concierge services, foreign currency exchange, housekeeping, dry-cleaning and laundry services, complimentary shoe shines, and a nightly turn-down service. There's even a complimentary late-night snack: a peanut butter and jelly sandwich on Texas toast and some cold milk.

The premier suite is the Cattle Baron's Suite, located on the mezzanine. Restoration of this magnificent area cost $300,000—more than the entire building, complete with furnishings, cost in 1886. Period furniture can be found throughout the room, and the seven different paint colors used give the suite a rich, warm, and masculine feel. The two-bedroom suite is the Driskill's signature. It's where governors and heads of state—including Bill and Hillary—have stayed.

Of course, at $2,500 a night, it isn't for everyone.

On the opposite end of the mezzanine sits the Heritage Suite, with a less masculine look about it and a small balcony overlooking downtown Austin. Price tag? $1,000 a night.

Built in the 1880s, the famous Driskill Hotel combines elegance, Texana, and a prime Austin location.

Not that everything's this costly at the Driskill. Rooms start at $225.

For meetings, weddings, and special events, the hotel has some 15,000 square feet of meeting space. The mezzanine is prime for wedding and social functions. The highlight might be the 1,500-square-foot Maximilian Room with original chandeliers (relamped for electricity) and eight mirrors that the Mexican emperor gave his wife, Carlotta, as a wedding present. The mirrors were discovered by the Driskill's owners in the early 1900s in a San Antonio warehouse. The Driskill Ballroom, with 2,501 square feet, showcases the trompe l'oeil skylight, etched glass doors, and several murals.

The Driskill "D" can be found throughout the hotel—from the thresholds to the carpet—along with original artwork, antiques, and ceiling fans. Texas artists were used as much as possible, although the carpet work was crafted in England.

All of this eye-popping wandering might work up an appetite, but don't think all the Driskill offers in the food department is a glass of milk and a PB&J.

The Driskill Grill features the work of noted executive chef David J. Bull. Breakfast, lunch, and dinner are offered daily, and a Sunday brunch is always a hit. Food ranges from blackened salmon fillet to a barbecue duck burrito.

If you're thirsty, the Driskill Bar is a popular watering hole, with a tongue-in-cheek cowboy flavor from the Driskill D carpet to the mounted longhorn over the fireplace to the bronze sculpture *The Widowmaker*, which depicts a cowboy attempting to save the life of his pard, who has been thrown from his galloping horse and, with boot caught in the stirrup, might be dragged to death unless his pard can shoot the runaway horse with his Winchester.

That might sound and look a little morbid, but it's definitely Texas. The bar also features nightly entertainment and a coppered ceiling.

With a staff of about 200, the Driskill can match its splendor with personal service. A rooftop swimming pool and a fitness room are scheduled to be completed by the fall of 2000. And no matter what you desire in a Texas hotel, the Driskill will fill the bill. As Tracy Fitz points out:

"You have the formality of the lobby, the grandeur of the mezzanine, the B&B feel in the rooms, and a very Texan bar and grill."

Cowboy Savvy

You couldn't ask for a better location than the Driskill. Austin's Sixth Street might be the best-known entertainment district in Texas, featuring restaurants and honky-tonks showcasing every kind of music imaginable. You can even find a tattoo parlor if you're so inclined. The Warehouse District is also nearby.

The hotel offers valet parking for guests, and other parking facilities are nearby.

The Driskill Hotel at a Glance

Address: 604 Brazos St., Austin, TX 78701

Phone: (512) 474-5911, (800) 252-9367

Fax: (512) 474-2214

E-mail: information@driskillhotel.com

Internet: www.driskillhotel.com

Location: Downtown Austin.

Accommodations: 205 rooms and suites.

Dining: The Driskill Grill is open for breakfast, lunch, and dinner daily and Sunday brunch.

Rates: $225-$2,500. Corporate, group, and special rates available on request based on availability. Restrictions apply.

Credit cards: All.

Handicap access: Yes.

Smoking: Yes.

Pets: Yes, with $50 pet fee. Pet-sitter required if unattended.

Things to do: Location, location, location. Near the State Capitol, shores of Town Lake, and Austin's famous Sixth Street entertainment district.

Season: Open all year.

The Gage Hotel
Marathon

The Gage Hotel has seen 'em all, from lavish weddings to honeymooners, from actor Clint Eastwood to Big Bend National Park visitors looking for a restroom.

It's elegant and rustic rolled into one.

For many families, staying at The Gage is a vacation tradition.

"Some people request certain rooms," general manager Nelson Vansidener says. "Their mothers and daddies brought them to The Gage when they were kids and they stayed in a specific room, and now they're bringing their kids and want to stay in the same rooms."

Other travelers who drop in—Marathon sits at the intersection of U.S. Highways 90 and 385—on the way to the national park stand in awe at the furnishings. The paintings on the wall, the furniture, rugs, etc., aren't fakes. This is the real McCoy (all right; that's not an original Frederic Remington hanging in the suite in the Los Portales section of the hotel).

Check out the old John Wayne saddle, valued at $12,000, in one of the living areas. Those paintings in the dining room? They're worth between $12,000 and $26,000. And then there's the leather sofa, straight from the set of *Giant*. The epic 1956 motion picture starring Rock Hudson, Elizabeth Taylor, and

James Dean (who died before filming was completed) was filmed in and around Marfa. The sofa was part of an interior set in Hollywood that served as the Hudson-Taylor ranch house. Now it's time for movie trivia. Remember Mercedes McCambridge, who played Hudson's domineering sister, Luz? (She was nominated for an Academy Award by the way.) Well, not to give anything away if you haven't seen the movie, but Luz meets an untimely end in this epic and bites the bullet on a leather sofa.

This is the sofa.

Guess who made it?... Ralph Lauren. Seriously, unless Vansidener was pulling my leg when he told me.

The Gage owes its unique flavor to owner J.P. Bryan of Houston, a Western aficionado or, as better described by Vansidener, "really a cowboy who's an oilman."

J.P. and Mary Jon Bryan bought The Gage in 1978 and began a renovation process to turn the place into the premier hotel in West Texas and one of the best loved in the entire state.

The Gage Hotel: The Past

The Gage owes its vision to its original builder, San Antonio businessman/banker/rancher Alfred Gage, who had a sprawling ranch in the Marathon Basin of West Texas. A native of Vermont, Gage came west to seek his fortune in 1878. He cowboyed around West Texas and eventually founded the Alpine Cattle Company with his brothers. By 1920 a rather wealthy Alfred Gage saw the need to build a hotel in Marathon that could serve as a meeting place as well as his ranch headquarters.

Gage hired the El Paso architectural firm Trost and Trost, which would also design the once-renowned Paisano Hotel in Marfa. (Movie trivia, part 2: The Paisano served as headquarters for *Giant* during filming in the summer of 1955.) Trost and Trost designed the hotel, which was built by Ponfords and Sons of El Paso. The Gage opened for business in 1927; Alfred Gage died the following year.

Local ranchers, miners, and merchants met at The Gage, and as the Big Bend became a popular tourist destination, the hotel became an oasis.

The Bryans wanted to recapture that flavor when they bought the hotel.

The Gage Hotel: The Present

The hotel is divided into two buildings. The historic building, made of brick, has rooms with or without private baths. Rooms with baths are priced at $85, $20 more than those without. Don't be alarmed at having to share a bathroom, though. You'll find a nice ($100) terrycloth robe in your room, and the bathrooms down the hall are roomy and nicely done. Showers are private.

Note the transom windows above the doorways in the historic rooms, a throwback to the days before air conditioning. All rooms are completely air-conditioned these days.

The other part of The Gage is the modern adobe Los Portales, where you'll find the outdoor swimming pool and a verdant courtyard. Keeping things green in this desert is the job of Janice Jobe. I'm not sure how she does it—hey, this is a desert—but the flowers, including beautiful roses with a satin texture, are exquisite, and the courtyard is often decorated with *ristras*, wreaths or strings of dried chili peppers.

Rooms in Los Portales, which opened in 1992, come with ($140) or without ($120) fireplaces, or you can opt for the $175 suite. Firewood is provided. You'll find telephones in the new addition but not in the historic rooms. Telephones in the rooms, by the way, do not allow international calls (those must be made from pay phones).

"This is a very serene area," Vansidener says of Los Portales (Spanish for "The Porches"). The courtyard between the historic hotel and Los Portales is an excellent spot for dances, dinners, weddings, or cocktail parties. Warm yourself by the fire pit in the

The Gage Hotel was built in the 1920s as a gathering place and watering hole, and its popularity hasn't decreased.

winter, or relax by the pool in the summer. Remember: There is no lifeguard on duty.

Cafe Cenzio opened in 1996. Before that, visitors dined in what is now a small room that adjoins the lobby. The old dining room has a briefing table (original and antique, of course) that would take about six people to move. The meeting room can accommodate small parties.

The current restaurant is actually several sections, including an outdoor patio. Prices aren't cheap, but the servings are huge. The cheapest meal on the dinner menu is the vegetable platter at $14.95. A chicken-fried steak will run you $15.95 and a rib eye $25.95, or you might opt for the quail ($20.95). Whatever you do, save room for dessert ($4.25-$4.50), all made from scratch at the hotel. Breakfast prices are reasonable at $4.50 to $5.95, and comment cards are handed out for patrons along with the check.

A Civil War-era sniper's rifle rests on the wall, along with other expensive original paintings, and you'll likely find a fire going in the fireplace.

FYI: There is no room service at the hotel, and restaurant hours vary.

If you want to quench your thirst, the White Buffalo Cantina is a small but cozy watering hole (blue laws are in effect on Sundays). This isn't your ordinary gin joint. The bar is well named. That's a rare albino buffalo head mounted on the wall. American Indians put much spiritual value on white buffalo, and they still do. The buffalo head has to be one of the most photographed objects at The Gage (along with the wall of cow skulls outside the cafe).

With a full-time staff of fifty-seven, The Gage aims to please. Somewhere, Alfred Gage, who didn't really get a chance to enjoy his creation, must be pleased.

Cowboy Savvy

Weather is unpredictable in West Texas. I elected to dine outside at The Gage one evening when my wife and I were vacationing. Thunderheads were gathering, and our hostess asked if we preferred indoors. But this wasn't the rainy season, and I knew these clouds were probably just teasers. We sat outside and were enjoying our cocktails and appetizers when there came a loud crack of thunder, the wind picked up instantly, and the rain fell. The hostess moved us to an inside table and didn't laugh, not in front of us, at least.

The Gage Hotel at a Glance

Address: P.O. Box 46, Marathon, TX 79842
Phone: (800) 884-4243
Fax: (915) 386-4510
E-mail: welcome@gagehotel.com
Internet: www.gagehotel.com

Location: north side of U.S. Highway 90 in town.

Accommodations: 37.

Dining: Cafe Cenizo open for breakfast (6-10 A.M.
Monday-Friday, 7-11 A.M. Saturday), dinner (6-9 P.M.
Sunday-Thursday, 6-10 P.M. Friday-Saturday) and Sunday
brunch (7 A.M.-1 P.M.)

Rates: $65-$175.

Credit cards: American Express, Discover, MasterCard, Visa.

Handicap access: One room.

Smoking: No.

Pets: Yes (small).

Things to do: White Buffalo Cantina on site. Swimming pool.
Walking distance to shopping. Gage Tours can arrange
individual and group trips. Historic Ritchey Brothers
Center can accommodate meetings of up to 300 people.

Season: Open all year.

The Hotel Limpia

Fort Davis

Victorian-style rooms, brightly colored walls, long draperies, oatmeal soap, a glassed-in veranda, and relaxing gardens.... This is an Old West hotel?

Exactly. And it's one of the finest and most popular stops in West Texas.

The Hotel Limpia offers just about everything (except breakfast and lunch), from rocking chairs on the porch to comfortable beds with more pillows than you can shake a stick at. Gift shops, a bookstore, a restaurant that serves dinner (and Sunday brunch), and the only club where you can get a cold one in town are on site.

In addition to the historic hotel, circa 1913, the Limpia operates three other downtown guesthouses for travelers.

Hotel Limpia: The Past

Named after the nearby creek (meaning "clean"), the Hotel Limpia opened its doors in 1884 as a brick building near the Overland Trail and Fort Davis. The military abandoned the post in 1891, but by the turn of the century Fort Davis had become a summer tourist town. East Texans flocked from the heat and humidity to enjoy the mountain climate.

A larger, modern hotel was needed, so in 1912 the Union Trading Company built a two-story structure near the courthouse and bank. The new, improved Hotel Limpia opened in 1913 and did well serving Texans through the 1920s and '30s. Of course, when air conditioning came about in the '40s, the summer tourism trade began to suffer.

In 1953 a fire destroyed the hotel lobby. J.C. Duncan bought the hotel, remodeled it, and opened the first-floor space to Harvard University's radio-astronomy interests. The rest of the building was turned into apartments. Twenty-five years later, Duncan decided to turn the building back into a hotel, complete with central heat and air and private baths. The next new, improved Hotel Limpia opened its doors on July 2, 1978.

J.C. Duncan died in 1982, and the hotel changed hands as it was leased, sold, and returned to the family through foreclosure. Its future seemed in doubt until Duncan's son, Joe, and daughter-in-law, Lanna, expressed an interest in buying the building.

"They thought we were crazy," Joe Duncan says. "But we felt with sweat equity, good ideas, and hard work, we could turn this around and make it work."

Joe and Lanna took over in 1991, and the Limpia's future seems brighter than ever.

Hotel Limpia: The Present

Joe had been in commercial real estate in Dallas, while Lanna worked as a counselor in the Highland Park school district. The Limpia wasn't in peak condition when they bought it, but the couple went to work with a passion. Today they have a staff of forty to help them out.

Rooms in the historic hotel feature ceiling fans and televisions (but no phones), with 12-foot-high ceilings made of ornamental pressed tin, and transom windows. The furniture helps transform these old rooms into a romantic getaway. Lanna Duncan missed her calling. She could have made a fortune as an interior decorator.

The historic hotel features ten standard rooms and three suites, while the Limpia West, a 1920s annex, has eight rooms with reproduction turn-of-the-century furniture. Guests may opt to stay in one of the historic homes. The 1905 adobe Mulhern House, which the Limpia opened in 1997, has three suites, porch, and a yard shaded by fruit and pecan trees. The circa 1940 Etheridge Cottage is located on three acres that border Fort Davis National Historic Site. The three-suite Dr. Jones House, circa 1903, is on two acres at the edge of Sleeping Lion Mountain. Complimentary coffee is available each morning in the hotel lobby.

Peak season is spring and fall. The Hotel Limpia also takes part in an elder-hostel program 30 weeks each year. So it's always advisable to make reservations early.

The restaurant is the nicest in town. Expect to pay between $4 and $6 for appetizers and $9 to $19 for entrees. Specials are offered daily. Portions are not huge, but the food is excellent.

This is a dry precinct, but the hotel's Sutler's Club is open for membership. Hotel guests receive a complimentary membership during their stay. Temporary ($3 for four people and three days) and annual ($25) memberships are available. One note if you're staying at the hotel and want a cocktail: The state policy requires hotel guests to charge alcoholic beverages to their room. This includes food purchases with alcohol.

Enjoy your stay. As Joe Duncan points out, Fort Davis "is a good place to raise children." And it's an excellent place to visit.

Hotel Limpia is a charming Victorian getaway in a historic frontier hotel.

Cowboy Savvy

If you wake up hungry, remember there's no breakfast served at the Limpia. Not to worry. Just across Main Street (Highway 17) sits the Old Texas Inn, home of Texas-size biscuits, traditional breakfast, and a good cup of Joe at a modest price. Don't expect fancy dining accommodations—in fact, those benches can be downright uncomfortable—but the food will fill you up. If you sleep in, the full-service restaurant also features an old-fashioned soda fountain, as well as a gift shop. The Old Texas Inn is just that, too, so if the Limpia is booked, you might call the Inn at (800) DAVIS-MT or (915) 426-3118 for hotel reservations.

The Hotel Limpia at a Glance

Address: P.O. Box 1341, Fort Davis, TX 79734

Phone: (800) 662-5517, (915) 426-3237

Fax: (915) 426-3983

E-mail: frontdesk@hotellimpia.com

Internet: www.hotellimpia.com

Location: east side of Highway 17 in town.

Accommodations: 39 in four buildings downtown.

Dining: Restaurant open Tuesday-Sunday 5:30-9:30 P.M. and for Sunday brunch 11 A.M.-2 P.M.

Rates: $69-$150.

Credit cards: All.

Handicap access: No.

Smoking: No.

Pets: Yes.

Things to do: Hotel Limpia gift store and Javelinas and Hollyhocks nature store on site. Sutler's Club is only full-service bar in town.

Season: Open all year.

Indian Lodge

Davis Mountains State Park, Fort Davis

You might say Indian Lodge is for families who want to go camping without actually camping. It's located in one of Texas's best state parks, and it's an easily affordable full-service hotel, complete with swimming pool, gift shop, and restaurant.

The architecture is Southwestern/pueblo, and the rooms have a rustic, Southwestern decor. But don't start a fire in the kiva fireplace! It's there just for show. And keep the young'uns off the roof. Pueblo-style buildings aren't made for roof dancing.

This isn't what you expect to find at a park hotel. Forget about some roughshod cabin with an uncomfortable bed, but don't take my word for it. In 1992 *Texas Highways* magazine readers voted the Lodge the No. 1 accommodation in the state.

Book early, too. Especially during peak season, Indian Lodge can fill up fast. You can pick up a pass at the park entrance if you're simply staying at the Lodge, or buy a entry permit to the park's recreation features if you want to rough it as well as relax.

Indian Lodge: The Past

In 1933 the Civilian Conservation Corps completed a fifteen-room, three-level hotel in the state park. The landscape featured a courtyard with an outdoor fireplace and desert gardens. Thirty-four years later the Texas Parks and Wildlife Department renovated the original rooms and built twenty-four additional rooms, the swimming pool, and the Black Bear Restaurant.

In the Southwestern tradition, rooms, with walls eighteen to twenty-two inches thick, have ceilings of pine *vigas* and river-cane *rajas*. Much of the furniture is the Lodge's original hand-hewn cedar.

Indian Lodge: The Present

The rooms today blend the tradition of the old Lodge with modern amenities. Floors are carpeted, and rooms are equipped with central cooling and heating, telephones, and televisions with remote control.

Full maid service is offered, and the Lodge has two meeting rooms.

The Black Bear Restaurant serves burgers, the omnipresent chicken-fried steak, and Tex-Mex fare. FYI: The restaurant is run separately so don't expect to charge your meals to your room, but

Indian Lodge is a pueblo-style hotel located in Davis Mountains State Park.

credit cards are accepted. Service might be a little slow, too, but, hey, you're in the Davis Mountains. Relax.

This is family dining, and since many vacationers bring their children with them, you might find the restaurant and lodge a little noisy. Besides, how many restaurants do you know where they serve Big Red? I told you it's geared for families and children.

The best part of Indian Lodge is the location. Davis Mountains State Park sports 2,700 acres. Take a hike and watch for wildlife. Montezuma quail, deer, javelina, and antelope roam these hills, and there's plenty of desert fauna. If you're lucky, you might watch a full moon rise over the mountains and brighten the landscape.

Best of all, when you're finished communing with nature, you don't have to sleep in a tent pitched on rocky ground.

Cowboy Savvy

The best trail at Davis Mountains State Park is the five-mile path from the park campground down into Fort Davis Historical Site. The old fort is certainly worth a trip, and if you're not up to a five-mile hike, get in the car and drive. Admission is $2, and the park is open from 8 A.M. to 5 P.M. between early September and late May, and 8 A.M. to 6 P.M. the rest of the year. It is closed Christmas. From 1867 to 1885 Fort Davis was home to the Tenth Cavalry, one of the famous Buffalo Soldiers regiments of black enlisted men and (usually) white officers. You'll find an excellent museum at the visitor center and a knowledgeable and friendly staff.

Indian Lodge at a Glance

Address: P.O. Box 1458, Fort Davis, TX 79734
Phone: (915) 426-3254
Fax: (915) 426-2022
E-mail: N/A

Internet: N/A

Location: In Davis Mountains State Park on Park Road 3, 3 miles northwest of Fort Davis on Highway 118.

Accommodations: 39 guestrooms.

Dining: Full-service Black Bear Restaurant open for breakfast, lunch, dinner. Hours vary depending on season.

Rates: $55-$85, based on 1-2 adults, each additional adult $10. Children under 12 free. Rollaway beds available for $15 per night.

Credit cards: Discover, MasterCard, Visa.

Handicap access: Yes.

Smoking: Yes.

Pets: No.

Things to do: Gift shop, swimming pool. State park offers hiking trails, camping, picnic areas, etc.

Season: Closed the second Monday through fourth Monday each January.

The Nutt House Hotel

Granbury

The Nutt House Hotel on Granbury's historic square is an interesting piece of business. The downstairs is home to the Hennington Cafe; the upstairs is the hotel. Two businesses, two owners, one building.

The food downstairs is popular among tourists, and the Nutt House Hotel is one of the best places to stay in town and easily affordable ($57 to $125 a night).

Nine small rooms and one suite have the flavor of a 1919 hotel. The screen doors slam, which always seems to remind manager Cindi Meehan of "Mama saying, 'Don't let that door—SLAM!—slam!' "

Nutt House Hotel: The Past

Jim Warren built the hotel in 1893 for Jacob and Jesse Nutt, whose first store in Granbury was a small log cabin with a wagon yard, established in 1866. The Nutt brothers, who were blind, had helped Granbury secure the county seat. Warren used stone quarried from Hood County to build the two-story structure.

The Nutt House has been operating as a hotel continuously since about 1911.

Nutt House Hotel: The Present

The suite has a full kitchen and private bathroom. It can sleep up to six, so it's perfect for families. The other nine rooms share three baths, but all rooms have running water.

Breakfast is served continental-style, with juices, pastry, fruits, and coffee or tea.

Make no mistake. These rooms are small, but the beds are comfortable, and no one wants to spend a lot of time in a hotel room while in Granbury.

This town features the Brazos Drive-In Theater, one of the few remaining 1950s-style drive-ins still operating in Texas; the circa 1886 Granbury Opera House; and several museums and historic homes (not to mention a lot of shopping and dining opportunities). You can take a carriage ride (with bells on for Christmas) around the square, or you can arrange for longer tours. The guides will even show you Jesse James's grave. Most historians will agree that Bob Ford, that "dirty little coward," killed Jesse James in 1882 in Missouri. But Granbury boasts that the outlaw died here in 1951 at the age of 104. Granbury also suggests that John Wilkes Booth wasn't killed in 1865 but worked here for a spell.

My thoughts on the matter? Elvis is dead.

The Nutt House Hotel offers a prime place to rest up before and after antique shopping in Granbury.

Outlaws and assassins notwithstanding, the Nutt House Hotel and downtown Granbury manage to cast a spell on visitors. The Nutt House Hotel may not be the most glamorous hotel in Texas, but it's certainly full of charm.

Weekends generally attract a crowd, so the midweek might be the best time to enjoy the Nutt House and Granbury. "Granbury is a quiet place," Cindi Meehan says, "quiet and peaceful." And so is the Nutt House—even when those screen doors slam.

Cowboy Savvy

If you're interested in antiques and reproductions, check out The Wagon Yard (213 N. Crockett) behind the Nutt House Hotel. Ten rooms are filled with furniture and just about everything you can imagine. The store is open Monday through Saturday from 8:30 A.M. to 5:30 P.M., and the first and third Sundays of each month from noon to 5 P.M. For information, call (817) 573-5321.

The Wagon Yard is part of Granbury's history, too. It was originally just that—a wagon yard—and travelers would park their wagons here before checking into the old hotel.

The Nutt House Hotel at a Glance

Address: 121 E. Bridge St., Granbury, TX 76049
Phone: (817) 279-9457
Fax: (817) 573-2709
E-mail: N/A
Internet: N/A
Location: On the square in historical downtown.
Accommodations: Ten.
Dining: Continental breakfast.
Rates: $57 to $125.
Credit cards: American Express, Discover, MasterCard, Visa.
Handicap access: No.
Smoking: No.

Pets: No.

Things to do: Walking distance to shopping, restaurants, and live entertainment.

Season: Open all year.

Stockyards Hotel

Fort Worth

When former Confederate Colonel Thomas Marion Thannisch built the Stockyards Hotel in 1906-7, he envisioned a place that combined Old West charm with twentieth-century comforts. After all, this three-story building had ninety rooms and a bathroom on each floor.

Today, you'll find fifty-two rooms and suites—and each with a private bath. Rooms come in four styles: Native American, Cowboy, Mountain Man ("bring your own," the joke goes), and Victorian. Suites include the Butch Cassidy and Cattle Baron.

Let's not forget the Celebrity Suite, either, because the Stockyards Hotel has entertained its share of celebrities, from Tanya Tucker and Pam Tillis (Billy Bob's, Fort Worth's famous honkytonk, is just around the corner) to duos such as Brooks and Dunn, the country-music singers, and Bonnie and Clyde, *the* Bonnie and Clyde.

Stockyards Hotel: The Past

The Colonel's creation was the first brick building in Fort Worth's Stockyards. The eastern portion is the original structure, and the western part is an addition completed in 1914. Originally a ninety-room hotel, the first floor housed merchants such as jewelers and barbers. Thannisch's block building was a wonder, with a corbeled parapet and artsy brickwork, complete with chevron designs in the top story. Thannisch died in 1935.

In 1933 Clyde Barrow and Bonnie Parker slept here while on the run from the law. They picked a corner room on the third floor with a good view of Main Street and Exchange Avenue in case they needed to make a quick getaway.

Later guests weren't as famous as the Depression-era bank robbers. The magnificent Stockyards Hotel deteriorated into a flophouse, catering to roughnecks and an ungainly clientele. Garbage was dumped into the alleys. It was a dangerous area. You could rent a room for $25 a week, but who would want to?

That changed when Fort Worth began efforts to clean up the Stockyards district and turn it into a tourist mecca. Billy Bob's opened in the early 1980s, and the Hotel was reborn in 1983. Today, the Stockyards is one of the premier entertainment/shopping/dining districts in the West, and the Stockyards Hotel is the premier place to stay.

Stockyards Hotel: The Present

The rooms and suites may look rustic (with the wooden shutters made of wormwood), but they come complete with televisions, phones, ironing boards, and other modern conveniences, most of them hidden in armoires. Speaking of those shutters, legend has it that the holes in some of them are byproducts of the days when the Stockyards catered to poker games and violent quarrels). Artwork and decor reflect the themes of each room. The Bonnie and Clyde room (room 305, by the way) includes newspaper clippings and photographs of the outlaws, who were gunned down in Louisiana and buried in Dallas. The Geronimo (much more Arizona, New Mexico, and Oklahoma than Texas) pays tribute to the Apache warrior, and the Davy Crockett room comes with—what else!—a coonskin cap.

In the Celebrity Suite, you'll find a bar, deck, stereo system (not an 8-track, by any means), and a hot tub that, according to the brochure, is a favorite of country-music stars (how do they know?).

The Longhorn and Quanah Parker rooms are perfect for meetings and banquets. The steer-head carpet throughout the hotel was custom-made in England, and the wallpaper is real suede. The wall sconces are also custom.

The bathrooms are old-fashioned water closets. Don't let the name fool you. These "closets" are large, complete with big tubs (the only Jacuzzi, though, is in the Celebrity suite, and there is no swimming pool on the site). And you don't have to share your bathroom with the other guests on the same floor as travelers did in 1907.

Fort Worth's Stockyards Hotel once housed Bonnie and Clyde, but now caters to a less violent element.

Valet parking is the way to go. A side note: Stockyards-area streets are closed for various annual celebrations, including Memorial Day weekend, Chisholm Trail Roundup (June), Pioneer Days (September), and the Red Steagall Cowboy Gathering and

Western Swing Festival (October). Check with the Fort Worth Convention & Visitors Bureau (800-433-5747, 817-336-8791, www.fortworth.com) for details.

Texas grub can be had at the Hunter Brothers' H3 Ranch, which features a hickory wood grill. A chicken-fried steak runs $11.95, or you can opt for the 40-ounce bone-in sirloin at $32.95. The price of the King Crab legs, however, depends on the crab's disposition. At least, that's what the menu says. The pork ribs ($5.95) are a pretty good appetizer considering this is a state known for its beef and not pig meat. Maybe the ribs are tasty because pigs, and sheep, were also sold at the Stockyards just down the street.

If you're thirsty (you can get a giant schooner and other refreshments at H3 Ranch, too), Booger Red's Saloon is popular. Named for a Texas bronc buster, Booger Red's features a belt-driven fan system and saddle-top barstools. I'm not sure if the bartenders will laugh at you, however, if you're bucked off one of them boogers.

Cowboy Savvy

Just across the street from the Stockyards is the White Elephant Saloon, a noted honky-tonk (don't call 'em bars around here, pard) that features live music seven nights a week. The White Elephant was the site of Cowtown's most famous shootout.

On February 8, 1887, Timothy Isaiah "Longhaired Jim" Courtright, a former marshal of Fort Worth, got into a ruckus with gambler Luke Short, part of the Dodge City gang. Courtright was demanding protection fees, which Short declined to pay. Legend has it that Short acted as though he were smoothing his vest and pulled his revolver. Courtright never got off a shot and was buried in Oakwood Cemetery. Six years later Short joined him there.

Of course, the original White Elephant was located in Fort Worth's notorious Hell's Half Acre, which is where you'll find the Convention Center these days. But the new White Elephant is the perfect place to experience Cowtown's nightlife, complete with a long wooden bar with brass foot rail, and a collection of hats hanging on the ceiling and walls.

The Courtright-Short gunfight, by the way, is reenacted on the anniversary of the shootout at the saloon. Pssst. Don't bet on Longhaired Jim.

Stockyards Hotel at a Glance

Address: 109 E. Exchange Ave., Fort Worth, TX 76106

Phone: (817) 625-6427, (800) 423-8471

Fax: (817) 624-2571

E-mail: jvara@stockyardshotel.com

Internet: www.stockyardshotel.com

Location: 2.5 miles north of downtown Fort Worth in the Stockyards National Historic District.

Accommodations: 52.

Dining: Hunter Brothers' H3 Ranch serves lunch and dinner daily, and breakfast Saturdays and Sundays.

Rates: $115 to $350.

Credit cards: All.

Handicap access: No.

Smoking: Yes.

Pets: Yes (with $50 nonrefundable deposit).

Things to do: Hunter Brothers' H3 Ranch restaurant, Booger Red's Saloon, The Main Exchange gift shop on premises. Walking distance to other shopping, dining, and honky-tonks. No swimming pool.

Season: Open all year.

Y.O. Ranch Resort Hotel and Conference Center

Kerrville

"It's unique," Fay Faure, senior sales manager for the Y.O. Ranch Resort Hotel and Conference Center, says. "I like it."

What's not to like?

There's certainly enough space: a 6,000-square-foot lobby filled with game trophies, sculptures, Western artifacts, and chandeliers decorated with branding irons; 200 guestrooms; and meeting space totaling 11,000 square feet.

There's plenty to do, with an awesome saloon, lighted tennis court, exercise facilities, outdoor pool (with swim-up bar), sauna, gift shop, outdoor amphitheater, and playground for children.

There's the location: The hotel is a block off Interstate 10 in the heart of the beautiful Texas Hill Country.

And you can't forget the history. The walls are full of history, including the framed pages of *Harper's Weekly*, *Frank Leslie's Illustrated*, and other old magazines. That's fitting. The hotel's namesake is one of the most famous ranches in Texas.

Y.O. Ranch Resort Hotel: The Past

The hotel was built in 1984 by the Schreiner family, which has owned the famous Y.O. Ranch, located just down the road near Mountain Home, since 1880. The eight-building hotel was made of native limestone, with the guest units named after Texas creeks and rivers (Bear Creek, Pecos, Rio Grande, Colorado, Paint Creek, Johnson Fork, Red River). In the mid-1990s, Holiday Inn bought the hotel. Of course, the Y.O. wasn't your typical Holiday Inn.

Its Western roots were easily spotted, from the covered wagon parked out front to the mounted trophies on the walls to the massive fireplace in the lobby.

In January 2000 the Gal-Tex Hotel Corporation bought the Y.O. Hotel. The Galveston, Texas-based company owns and manages seventeen facilities, including the historic Menger and Crockett Hotels in San Antonio.

Gal-Tex plans to restore the hotel's rich heritage.

That shouldn't be a hard job.

Y.O. Ranch Resort Hotel: The Present

Let's start with those five massive chandeliers in the lobby. Each is nine feet wide and adorned with actual branding irons from Texas ranches.

The guest units surround the outside patio, which features the swimming pool (the swim-up bar is called The Jersey Lilly), spa, and the so-called "corral," perfect for barbecues or a dance.

Throughout the hotel, the floors are Saltillo tile. Rooms vary in size, but all include climate control, cable television, ironing board, oversize closets, and coffeemaker. Check out the pedestal sinks in the bathrooms.

You have your choice of king-size bed, two queen-size beds, executive guest quarters, or suite parlors with optional adjoining bedrooms. Some rooms have fireplaces and bars. All of them feature the Western art and decor showcased throughout the hotel.

Bringing the children with you? You might consider one of the hotel's eight "kidsuites," appropriately labeled "Fort Kid." These suites include a bedroom for the children separated from the rest of the suite by a split-wood, well, fort. The children will have their own videocassette recorder, telephone, television and Nintendo (free), and bunk beds. "This is a new concept," Faure says, "and we're really kind of excited about it."

For adults, there's the Elm Waterhole Saloon—Elm Waterhole being the coolest part of the actual Y.O. Ranch. John Wayne would have enjoyed this watering hole, with a thirty-foot antique mahogany bar and brass rail that Faure says is the longest continuous bar in Texas.

The massive lobby at the Y.O. Ranch Resort Hotel is filled with Western décor.

The Sam Houston Dining Room and Boon Bar has eighteen chandeliers and a marble bar from Chicago. The menu was being adjusted when I visited, but the full-service restaurant serves everything from ranch grub to wild game. After all, the Y.O. Ranch is known for its game.

Don't forget part of this hotel's name is "Conference Center." That means six meeting rooms—Live Oak Ballroom, Spanish Oak, Cypress, Live Oak, Boone, and Crockett—that can function for meetings of ten people to a thousand. The hotel offers a catering department as well.

The hotel's slogan is "Come Live the Texas Legend."

You'll certainly feel you're living that legend here.

Cowboy Savvy

Kerrville is home to the Cowboy Artists of America Museum, which sits on ten acres at 1550 Bandera Highway. In addition to a rotating art collection featuring bronzes, stone sculptures, and all types of Western paintings, the museum has a Western research library and a store where prints, books, videos, and other items can be bought. Youth and adult education programs are offered.

Admission fees are $5 for adults, $1 for children 6-18, $3.50 for senior citizens. There is no fee for museum members, and group rates are available.

The museum is open 9 A.M.-5 P.M. Monday through Saturday and 1-5 P.M. Sunday. It is closed New Year's Day, Easter, Thanksgiving, and Christmas Day. The mailing address is P.O. Box 1716, Kerrville, TX 78029-1716, phone (830) 896-2553, fax (830) 896-2556, website www.caamuseum.com.

The staff at the Y.O. Ranch Resort Hotel would be glad to answer any questions you might have about the museum.

"We try to promote the museum as much as possible," Faure says.

Y.O. Ranch Resort Hotel and Conference Center at a Glance

Address: 2033 Sidney Baker, Kerrville, TX 78028

Phone: (830) 257-4440

Fax: (830) 896-8189

E-mail: dosyo@ktc.com

Internet: www.yoresort.com

Location: 1 block south of Interstate 10 on State Highway 16.

Accommodations: 200 rooms and suites.

Dining: Sam Houston dining room, 6:30 A.M.-2 P.M., 5-10 P.M.

Rates: $49-$200.

Credit cards: All.

Handicap access: Yes.

Smoking: Yes.

Pets: Yes.

Things to do: Gift shop, hot tub, swimming pool (with swim-up
    bar), volleyball, basketball, walking/jogging track,
    playground. Saloon also on site.

Season: Open all year.

Ranches & Resorts

Bar H Dude Ranch

Clarendon

The name "Bar H Dude Ranch" might be a misnomer. Oh, make no mistake: This 5,500-acre spread in the Panhandle is a "dude" ranch. The old cowboy boots placed on top of fence posts and the cowboy pavilion perfect for barbecues and dances are dead giveaways.

But the Bar H is also a working cattle ranch, so instead of playing cowboy by going on hour-long trail rides and trying to sing like Don Edwards around campfires, guests here can actually learn what it's like to be a cowboy.

That means mending fences, feeding livestock, branding cattle, or even rounding up and moving them dogies along during the ranch's spring (May) and fall (September) cattle drives ($625 per adult).

Bar H Dude Ranch: The Past

The Panhandle has long been Texas cattle country. Charles Goodnight founded a ranch in Palo Duro Canyon in the 1870s, and the famous XIT Ranch was started in the 1880s. F.J. Hommel established the Bar H in the 1930s, and it remained a working ranch until Hommel's grandson, Frank, read an article in *Texas Highways* magazine in 1991 about the dude ranches in South Texas.

"It kinda intrigued me and I was curious about why there were none around here," Frank Hommel says. "So I loaded up in March or so and went to Bandera and looked around and talked to some of the guys around there, came back, got a chuck wagon, and started cooking meals in July of '91."

The first rooms were ready that fall, and the Bar H had about 500 guests that season. In 1992 that number swelled to 4,000. Visitors have come from every state and sixty or seventy countries, Hommel says.

Bar H Dude Ranch: The Present

Don't expect to find a clock in your room at the Bar H. Real cowboys know that the aroma of coffee boiling over the fire is better than any alarm. After a filling breakfast of eggs, meat, biscuits, and gravy, it's time to go to work.

Ranch activities vary during the season. Working cowboys don't brand cattle every day, and since the Bar H is a bona fide ranch, work isn't provided for the entertainment of guests.

"We had a guy call yesterday wanting to go on a cattle drive this month," Hommel says one February afternoon. "Well, we're not doing anything like that this time of year."

This isn't just for city slickers, though. If you don't feel like paying to work, feel free to just watch and learn. Nor are you required to ride a horse. The Bar H provides wagons for ranch tours. You pick your own pace, whether it's working, watching, or simply relaxing. A swimming pool is open during the summer season, and a volleyball court, fishing hole, and place to pitch horseshoes are provided. Hiking along the creek is popular. Across the ranch, there are plenty of cattle and some buffalo to

These boots are made for fences (well, not really) at the Bar H Dude Ranch.

view, or if you're lucky you might see an armadillo, deer, or hawk.

In addition to ten rooms, the ranch can rent out a house filled with bunk beds, which is the ideal place for groups and families. After an evening meal, you can retire for a good night's rest so you'll be ready for another cowboy adventure—whether it's in the saddle or by the pool.

Cowboy Savvy

The Bar H caters to hunters during hunting season. Licensed by the Texas Parks and Wildlife Department, the ranch offers quail and deer hunting. The ranch is also open for reunions, weddings, and retreats.

Rates are variable, so guests can stay for one day or two weeks. It just depends on your budget and your backside (if you plan on sittin' in a saddle for a spell).

The ranch even welcomes guests who have only a few hours to kill and want to eat a real cowboy meal.

"We feed about 14,000 people a year," Hommel says. "That's a lot of mesquite firewood, I guarantee you. That's a lot of rib eye steaks."

Bar H Dude Ranch at a Glance

Address: P.O. Box 1191, Clarendon, TX 79226

Phone: (800) 627-9871, (806) 874-2634

Fax: (806) 874-3679

E-mail: barh@gte.net

Internet: www.tourtexas.com/barhduderanch/

Location: Three miles north of Clarendon on F.M. 3257 off U.S. Highway 287.

Accommodations: 10 rooms, 1 house (can accommodate up to 60 total).

Dining: Three meals included.

Rates: Adults $65-$75 daily and $425-$485 weekly. Ages 2-5
    $28 daily and $165 weekly, ages 6-11 $45 and $285, ages
    12-16 $55 and $365, children under 2 free.
Credit cards: American Express, MasterCard, Visa
Handicap access: One bunkhouse.
Smoking: Yes.
Pets: Small.
Things to do: Horseback riding, wildlife viewing, swimming
    pool in season, hunting, horseshoes, fishing, volleyball,
    ranch tours, ranch work.
Season: Open all year.

Cibolo Creek Ranch

Shafter

About 32 miles south of Marfa, in this rather rugged and deso-
late country, you would never guess you were so close to a
veritable oasis in the desert, let alone one of the most luxurious
resorts in the entire state. After all, this is 225 miles from Mid-
land and 214 miles from El Paso. But here you'll find Cibolo
Creek Ranch, a stunning hacienda that blends in perfectly with
the restored baronial fort, El Fortín del Cibolo, of West Texas
frontiersman Milton Faver.

This 25,000-acre ranch also includes other restored historic
structures built by Faver in the 1850s, La Ciénaga and La Morita.
The tomb of Faver sits on a hill overlooking the Cibolo grounds.
Longhorn cattle, buffalo, and other animals roam the grounds,
including the not-so-romantic javelinas and skunks.

Don't let those scare you off, though. Cibolo Creek has entertained celebrities such as Mick Jagger, Dan Rather, and Larry

Hagman. There's even a 5,300-foot airstrip on the ranch for private planes (a liability release is required before arrival).

Cibolo Creek Ranch is the perfect place to recharge your batteries. You set your own pace. The rooms are spacious and first class, and the staff is excellent. It's like finding a five-star hotel in the middle of nowhere.

Rates begin at $250 a night. That includes three meals and nonalcoholic beverages (beer and wine are available, at additional cost, but hard liquor must be supplied by guests).

I must point out that when I stayed at Cibolo Creek, the fabulous husband-wife duo of Arthur and Lisa Ahier served as managing director and chef, respectively. You couldn't hope to find better folks than the Ahiers. Artie is easy-going, knowledgeable, and entertaining, the perfect host who always makes you feel at home and one excellent birding guide; Lisa, a graduate of the Culinary Institute of America, serves the best meals in the world. However, Lisa and Artie decided to move on at the end of February 2000 after three years at the resort. Their boots can never be filled, but one can only hope that their replacements will continue Cibolo's exquisite tradition.

To fully enjoy your stay at Cibolo Creek, it helps to know a little history (there's an excellent library and museum in the restored Cibolo fort, too).

Cibolo: The Past

Water meant life in the parched Big Bend country of Far West Texas, especially in the 1850s. Milton Faver, a trader and merchant in present-day Ojinaga, Mexico (just across the Rio Grande from Presidio) knew this when he established his headquarters at El Fortín del Cibolo in the Chinati Mountains between Presidio and Fort Davis.

Faver himself is worth a book. He is called "The Mystery Man of the Big Bend," and the moniker is well deserved. He has been called a native Virginian, Kentuckian, Missourian . . . the theories go on. Some say he was towering; others say he was small. Legend has it that a young Faver fled Missouri, thinking he had killed a man in a duel. He wound up in Meoqui, Mexico, and began a trading venture. At some point, he learned the location of a series of springs in the Chinatis, and after the military established a post on Limpia Creek in the Davis Mountains in 1854, Faver decided to establish a ranch between the fort and Presidio.

The story is that Faver (known among the Mexican population as Don Meliton) learned the man he shot in the Missouri duel wasn't dead, allowing him to return to the United States. He moved to Texas with his wife and son and became one of the first ranchers in the Big Bend—and quite a successful businessman.

Construction of the first fort at Cibolo (meaning "buffalo") began in 1857. This was Indian country, and Faver built wisely. A 90-by-140-foot stone corral, three feet thick and four feet high, was formed to hold horses, burros, and oxen, while the living quarters were made of adobe and native timber. The walls were between 20 and 30 inches thick, with round, two-story towers on the southeast and northwest corners. An acequia irrigation system brought water to the compound. As soon as Cibolo was complete, Faver began construction of another fort, El Fortín de la Ciénaga (meaning "marshy place") at the spring near Ciénaga Creek. This square structure included two-story towers on the southwest and northeast corners with a main gate facing the cottonwood and Arizona ash trees to the south. Stock pens made of rock walls were built thirty yards southeast of the fort.

Four miles southwest of Ciénega, Faver built the last fort, La Morita ("the little muleberry tree") at another spring, El Ojo de la Morita. This was the smallest of the three, with one tower in the center of the east wall.

La Morita would serve as headquarters for Faver's sheep and goat operation. On June 30, 1875, Indians (or, as one version has it, Mexican bandits disguised as Indians) attacked Morita, killing Carmen Ramirez, Faver's brother-in-law, and kidnapping

Ramirez's wife and children. La Ciénega became the base of Faver's cattle operation. And El Fortín del Cibolo would serve as Faver's headquarters. It was here that he brewed and served his famous peach brandy (made from homegrown peaches).

That peach brandy must have been something. It has become almost as legendary at old Don Meliton himself.

And Faver never missed a beat. He is said to have broken out the brandy first during his trading ventures, letting his guests imbibe freely before the haggling began. Legend also has it that he never accepted paper money, only gold and silver, and demanded payment for each head of cattle as it was tallied instead of waiting for the final count.

Milton Faver died on December 23, 1889. An adobe mausoleum was erected over his grave at Cibolo. His tombstone, in Spanish, read:

En memoria a
Meliton Faver
Quien murio
el dia 23 de Deciembre
del ano 1889 a la una
de la tarde.
Si tuvo faltas que fueron obvios,
y presento solo sus buenas,
acciones.

The translation is: "In memory of Meliton Faver who died on December 23 of the year 1889 at one o'clock in the afternoon. If he had faults, let them be forgotten and only his good deeds remembered."

Cibolo: The Present

In 1987 John Poindexter helped form Southwestern Holdings Inc. in Houston to buy and develop a ranch. Poindexter decided on the historic Faver ranches and began a massive restoration process lasting seven years. The San Antonio architectural firm of Ford, Powell and Carson, with help from the Texas State Historical Commission, took on the task of restoring the historic structures as well as building a hacienda at Cibolo that would blend in with the original buildings.

Keep in mind that according to Poindexter, his original idea was to build a ranch he could call home (indeed, the hacienda is also his home, although he's often in Houston). Later he decided the buildings and history were too important to call his own, so he elected to turn Cibolo Creek Ranch into an upscale resort. The resort opened for business in 1993.

The restoration—actual cost remains a secret, but you can bet your boots Faver never saw that much gold and silver in his day—is amazing. All three fortíns are on the National Register of Historic Places. At Ciénega, the amenities are well hidden. An armoire serves as a false front that leads into a bathroom. Morita, the most remote, is a one-room guest cottage. The first time I visited, Artie Ahier suggested Morita as the perfect hideaway to write that great American novel.

Both spots are beautiful but off the beaten path in an off-the-beaten-path hunk of Texas. Ciénega and Morita are about a half-hour drive from the Cibolo fort and hacienda.

Most guests prefer the main hacienda at Cibolo. The air-conditioning system is hidden in authentic ceilings of *vigas* and *rajas*, typical of Southwestern architecture. Most guestrooms feature adobe fireplaces, and there's a giant bathroom (it's probably bigger than some houses) complete with a Jacuzzi and double shower in the master suite ($590).

Improved hiking trails lead to Milton Faver's tomb and the springs at all three forts. Skeet shooting, four-wheeler tours, and horseback riding can be arranged. If you're worn-out or tense, massages can be scheduled. For the corporate-minded, Cibolo has two meeting rooms that can hold thirty-six to fifty people. Televisions are found in common living areas, and phones are

Cibolo Creek Ranch offers elegant dining and excellent food in a historic location.

located in public areas except at Morita, where messages are taken at Ciénega. There's an exercise room near the pool at Cibolo.

The guided trail rides are fun. Don't expect to be put on Old Glue Bait. On two trail rides, I found the horses to be lively and pretty good cow horses. Half-day excursions seem to be the norm, although longer and shorter trips may be arranged. A trip to the ghost town of Shafter is interesting, or the wrangler might take you by some Indian sites, caves, or other springs. Riders must sign an insurance release and safety forms before saddling up.

Remember: This is high desert, so drink plenty of water.

If you're really lucky, perhaps there will be a star party. Mark Bridges, a former astronomer with the McDonald Observatory in Fort Davis, sometimes shows up with a not-your-ordinary telescope, powerful binoculars, and a personable attitude that children and adults will enjoy—even if it's a 5 A.M. showing of Jupiter or Saturn (check out the rings) or a lesson in the constellations. The lectures aren't always at such an early/late hour, though. With luck, he might be setting up right after dinner.

Coffee is ready by 8 A.M., with breakfast served from 8 to 9. The menu varies, but you can count on fresh fruit and fresh juice. Lunch is ready at noon, with dinner at 7:30 P.M. Meals are set by the staff, but special diet needs are taken into consideration. Most meals are served B&B-style with your other guests maybe on the veranda or perhaps inside the historic Cibolo fort, but private meals can be arranged. You'll be missing out if you elect to dine alone, though. Part of the fun is meeting the fellow travelers, especially if you're fortunate to be there when European visitors are ranch guests.

A word of caution about the road to Cibolo. The staff advises you not to make the drive after dark unless you are quite familiar with the road to the main hacienda. This is a winding, roller-coaster road, mostly gravel, without guardrails. Longhorn cattle roam free. There are two gates with electric push-button openers. The main entrance off U.S. Highway 67 is also easy to miss if you aren't familiar with the ranch. A rock wall lines the entrance on the west side of the highway. Look for the state historical markers. The entrance is about six miles north of Shafter ghost town, or 25 miles north of Presidio. Call first for directions, or arrange a pickup if you're coming via charter plane or train to Alpine, about 68 miles from the ranch.

Cowboy Savvy

Pssst. Believe it or not, the best time to visit Cibolo Creek Ranch might be late July or August. These are Hell Weeks throughout much of Texas, but it's the rainy season (usually) in this part of the state. This has to be one of West Texas's best-kept secrets: You'll often find the temperatures here in late summer about ten degrees cooler than you'll find in Dallas or elsewhere in Texas.

And few things can match a late afternoon thunderstorm in the high desert.

Cibolo Creek Ranch at a Glance

Address: P.O. Box 44, Shafter, TX 79850

Phone: (915) 229-3737

Fax: (915) 229-3653

E-mail: cibolo@brooksdata.net

Internet: www.cibolocreekranch.com

Location: 32 miles south of Marfa on U.S. Highway 67.

Accommodations: 11 at Cibolo with an eight-room expansion planned, 4 at Cienega, 1 at Morita.

Dining: All meals included. Beer and wine available. No liquor served.

Rates: Cibolo $250-$590, Cienega $250-$290, Morita $350. Prices reduced June through September.

Credit cards: American Express, Discover, MasterCard, Visa.

Handicap access: Yes, with limitation.

Smoking: No.

Pets: Yes (call first).

Things to do: Horseback rides, birding and nature trails, swimming pool, paddleboats in small pond, library/museum.

Season: Open all year.

Dixie Dude Ranch

Bandera

The cowboys look like cowboys. The cabins look like cowboy cabins. And the corral and barn? Man, the only thing missing here is Marshal Matt Dillon or The Virginian dodging the horse apples. In fact, some commercials have been filmed using the setting as a backdrop.

Clay and Diane Conoly have got this dude ranch business down pat. The Dixie Dude Ranch isn't a resort; it's strictly "dude," complete with horseback riding, swimming, dancing, singing, and the omnipresent hayrides.

About the only thing unfriendly around these parts is the latch to the gate in front of the office and grub headquarters. As one staffer told me: "We get our entertainment watching people try to figure out how to open the gate."

Dixie Dude Ranch: The Past

William Wallace Whitley was twenty-three years old when he bought a stock-raising ranch near Bandera in 1901. When he decided to herd "dudes" in addition to stock back in 1937, he asked his daughter and son-in-law, Billie and Dee Crowell, to run the 7UK outfit.

The ranch has been family run for five generations now, entertaining waddie-wannabes from Texas and the world. Clay Conoly took over in 1988, and the Dixie Dude Ranch continues to go strong. Although the Dixie remains a working ranch, breeding longhorns, it's primarily known for running several head of "dudes" each year.

Dixie Dude Ranch: The Present

The ranch rests on 725 acres of prime Hill Country real estate. There are plenty of hiking trails (maps are provided), prime for looking for fossils, arrowheads, wildlife, or bird watching. Also for your pleasure are a fishing hole (catch-and-release), a heated swimming pool, and other activities commonplace on Texas guest ranches: basketball, volleyball, table tennis, and horseshoes. Now, horseshoes I can understand, but did cowboys really play basketball, volleyball, and table tennis? Starting at center, at 6-foot-10 in his Tony Lamas with lifts ... Texas Jack Omohundro! Oh, well, there is a difference between "dudes" and waddies.

For sleeping quarters, the ranch offers twenty cottages, including two rooms in the main house. All guestrooms and cabins have private bathrooms, air conditioning, and either a fireplace or vented heat. Many rooms are family style, with two or more beds, but others are designed for one or two folks. Deluxe cabins provide more space. A full maid service is provided for all lodging accommodations.

Rates include lodging, two horseback rides per day, and three home-cooked meals. Most of the grub is served family style indoors, but the ranch also offers the occasional cowboy breakfast, served on the trail, Sunday fried chicken, and barbecues. Usually, there is no evening meal or entertainment on Sundays, but Bandera offers plenty of restaurants and pubs, er, saloons, including The Silver Dollar Saloon and The Cabaret Cafe and Dance Hall.

The weight limit for horseback riding is 250 pounds. Children under the age of six ride double with an adult. As is the case at most dude ranches, all trail rides are guided and at a walk or trot. Riding lessons are available.

Keep in mind that the Dixie Dude Ranch does not sell liquor, but feel free to bring your own red-eye.

The corral and barn at Dixie Dude Ranch definitely look like the real McCoy.

Cowboy Savvy

The only thing complicated about the Dixie Dude Ranch is the rate schedule. High season rates for adults are in effect March 1 through November 30 and major holidays. Children's rates remain the same all year. Group rates are available for fifteen or more guests. Deluxe rates are ten percent higher than the standard plan. There's a two-night minimum stay, and a three-night minimum June through August and major holidays. Guests can check in on any day, providing they have reservations, except on Sundays.

One final note: Quoted rates do not include tax and gratuities.

Dixie Dude Ranch at a Glance

Address: Ranch Road 1077, P.O. Box 548, Bandera, TX 78003

Phone: (800) 375-9255, (830) 796-4481

Fax: (830) 796-4481

E-mail: cccdixie@hctc.net

Internet: www.dixieduderanch.com

Location: 7 miles from Bandera off Ranch Road 1077.

Accommodations: 20 cabins, includes two rooms in main house.

Dining: 3 meals daily served family style, buffet, and outdoor cookouts.

Rates: Adults $82-$112 daily, $540-$748 weekly. Children: Ages 2-5 $30-$33 daily/$185-$203 weekly, ages 6-12 $50-$55/$325-$357, ages 13-16 $60-$66/$400-$440, under 2 free. Group rates available.

Credit cards: Discover, MasterCard, Visa.

Handicap access: Yes.

Smoking: Yes.

Pets: No.

Things to do: Fishing hole, basketball court, volleyball, horseshoes, hiking trails, table tennis, horseback riding, swimming.

Season: Open all year.

Flying L Guest Ranch

Bandera

Here's the place for the corporate cowboy.

Just south of Bandera the 742-acre Flying L Guest Ranch attracts individuals, families, and businessmen and women from all over the globe. Sure, you'll find the typical Western ghost town and plenty of horses, but the Flying L isn't exactly what you'd call a "dude" ranch.

"We're more of a resort," says Jean Ballard, director of sales, "with a Western flavor."

What separates the Flying L from the myriad guest ranches in Texas is that par-72 golf course on the property. And, folks, we're not talking about "cowboy golf," where the hazards are dried dung, the golf cart is a 13½-hand roan gelding, and par is whatever the trail boss says it is. This is an 18-hole championship course with blue, white, and red tees, a pro shop, driving range, and practice areas.

For some families, a trip to the Flying L is two vacations in one. Mom can go horseback riding with the kids, and Dad can play golf.

Flying L Guest Ranch: The Past

Jack Lapham, a retired U.S. Army Air Corps colonel, bought a 542-acre spread from Polish settlers in 1946. Lapham envisioned a "dude" ranch, but flying was still his primary love so he also built an airstrip and ran a flight school. You can still spot the airplane hangers from Lapham's days, and the story goes that his buddies would often fly in for some poker games.

Lapham turned to associates of Frank Lloyd Wright to design his Ranch Villas for guests, and the resort soon began attracting not only war heroes, the colonel's buddies, and city slickers wanting a taste of the West but celebrities as well. John Wayne

117

stayed here, and so did actors Slim Pickens, Chill Wills, and Robert Fuller. If the scenery looks familiar, maybe it's because *The Cisco Kid* television series was filmed on the ranch. Other guests have included country-western singers Willie Nelson, Tex Ritter, Jim Reeves, Ray Price, and Buck Owens.

The Flying L has been sold twice since Lapham's purchase, in 1984 and 1998, and has grown in size and reputation.

Flying L Guest Ranch: The Present

Today's Flying L is part resort, part conference center. The ranch has forty-two villas and a bunkhouse that can sleep thirty. The bunkhouse has nine bedrooms, two baths, and a common lounge, the prime spot for retreats and getaways. All of the villas have a Western decor and come with refrigerator, microwave, cable television, and telephone. Some suites have fireplaces. In others, you might find a whirlpool, covered patio, or deck. The ranch can accommodate 110 guests.

Meals are served buffet style in the Main House dining rooms, outdoors at San Julian Creek, or poolside. A continental breakfast is offered from 7-9:30 A.M. if you're up early, and regular buffet breakfast is available from 7:30-9:30 A.M. Lunch and dinner come from preplanned menus, but specialty menus are also available.

Two popular spots at the ranch are Creekside, where you'll rough it with no electricity or running water but still a great spot for an outdoor barbecue or some of that team building stuff; and Ghost Town, a pavilion prime for dancing and eating near the Flying L's rodeo arena and stables. Transportation is always done by hay wagon, unless it's raining.

Thirsty? Well, the Branding Iron Saloon—check out previous groups' brands on the walls—serves up cocktails, including a daily drink special.

If you're here on corporate business, the ranch has several meeting rooms. The cedar-lined Roy Rogers Room can seat up to

Corporate guests and families enjoy the cowboy experience at the Flying L Guest Ranch.

120 and has a wrap-around deck where you can sip coffee during a break or just gaze at the scenery. The 20-by-36-foot Dale Evans Room—what else would it be called, Frog or Gabby?—has a seating capacity of 60. Other meeting rooms include the Sitting Bull Room, with a giant stone fireplace and seating capacity of 65. For smaller groups, try the Bob Wills Room or the Hank Williams Room, but take note of the latter's location: It's next to the Pro Shop.

Since we're this close to the golf course, it's time to break the bad news. Rates include lodging, meals, a one-hour trail ride, entertainment, and use of all ranch facilities, such as bicycling and the heated pool and lighted tennis courts—everything but golf.

You'll have to pay extra to try out the 6,700-yard course. Greens fees vary depending on the season, but the course has several specials and discounts, including a lower rate for senior citizens (55 and up) Monday through Friday. The course's Spike-n-Spur Grill serves breakfast, lunch, dinner, and cocktails.

For other forms of entertainment, the Flying L can provide trick-roping shows, sing-alongs, dancing, and a Casino Night. There are shootouts (staged with blanks, I'm told) and hangings (not real, I'm told, unless you're one mean guest).

One of the most popular offerings is the Cowboy Olympics, featuring roping live steers off wooden horses, and a waddie's version of the shot put but that's not a shot you're tossing (think cow patty). The closing event is "Riding Out on a Rail."

You've probably guessed it by now, but as Jean Ballard points out, "Our team building is real fun. We're not real serious here."

Cowboy Savvy

Another family feature at the resort is the Flying L's emphasis on children. The parents can have some quality time alone, knowing that Jimmy and Janie are having fun. Children's activities include painting rocks, baking cookies, and lots of barbecues. There's even a petting area.

Sign-up lists for the following day's Kids' Activities are posted at the front desk.

Flying L Guest Ranch at a Glance

Address: P.O. Box 1959, Bandera, TX 78003

Phone: (830) 460-3001, (800) 292-5134; golf center (800) 646-5407, (830) 796-8466

Fax: (830) 796-8455

E-mail: sales@flyingl.com

Internet: www.flyingl.com

Location: South of Bandera off Highway 173 on Wharton Dock Road.

Accommodations: 42 villas, bunkhouse sleeps up to 30.

Dining: 3 meals daily.

Rates: $80-$125 per person.

Credit cards: American Express, Discover, MasterCard, Visa.

Handicap access: Yes.

Smoking: Restricted.

Pets: No.

Things to do: Horseback riding, hayrides, swimming, cycling, tennis. All ranch activities included except golf, which is extra.

Season: Open all year.

Guadalupe River Ranch Resort and Spa

Boerne

Cut to the chase: Any ranch fit for Olivia de Havilland is good enough for me.

Before you quip that the Academy Award-winning actress is known for her roles in *Gone With The Wind* and opposite swash-buckling Errol Flynn in adventure flicks such as *The Adventures of Robin Hood* and *Captain Blood*, let's not forget that Errol and Olivia made a few Westerns together, including *They Died With Their Boots On* and *Santa Fe Trail*. Now in the great scheme of things, the Flynn-de Havilland Westerns are left in the dust by *My Darling Clementine*, *The Naked Spur*, and a lot of other flicks. But de Havilland could certainly pick a rancho, and Guadalupe River Ranch Resort and Spa leaves a lot of Texas guest ranches in the dust, too.

Guadalupe River Ranch: The Past

Walter Napier, president of San Antonio's Alamo National Bank, built an 8,000-square-foot lodge made of fieldstone and

121

cedar just outside of Boerne near the Guadalupe River. Napier, in turn, sold his dream home to Olivia de Havilland, who used the spacious house as a Hollywood getaway. According to legend, Olivia sold her rancho after driving her Packard into a big rock. The ranch has had several owners since.

(The lodge, by the way, isn't the oldest building on the property. That distinction goes to the grotto, a small chapel built of stone in the early 1900s to honor the Virgin of Guadalupe.)

The ranch became a place for "dudes" in the fifties, then Broadway producer Walter Starcke bought it in the late 1970s, originally envisioning a place for artists before turning it into a corporate retreat. When Ed and Elisa McClure became part owners and managers of the ranch in 1994, they added some bed-and-breakfast plans the following year.

Today the 360-acre Guadalupe River Ranch is a corporate retreat, guest ranch, resort, spa, bed-and-breakfast, and genuine Great Place to Be. It's also a great place to eat, serving up the best breakfast, lunch, and supper you'll find anywhere close to San Antonio.

Guadalupe River Ranch: The Present

For businesses, the ranch offers 5,000 square feet of meeting space. Meeting supplies, from projectors to pens and pads, are also available. If you don't want to conduct meetings inside, that's fine, too, because natural areas are available such as The Pavilion, an 857-square-foot covered area, and no one wants to be stuck inside on a sunny day in the Hill Country. If team building's the agenda, the ranch offers supervised zip-line rides, ropes challenge courses, and other activities fit for a fit scout.

Forty-seven rooms are available—and with a staff of fifty-five you can almost guarantee excellent service—and the stone cottages are complete with telephones, private baths, great views, beautiful furniture, a coffeemaker, and bottled water service provided daily. What you won't find is a television. There's only one on the entire ranch. Cottages come with two double or queen beds, and several have balconies or screened-in porches. View Rooms have a private balcony, queen bed, and queen sleeper sofa. Riverview Rooms have private balconies and a two-room one-bath suite. The Governor's Palace is a two-room two-bath suite with king bed, queen sleeper sofa, Murphy bed, and outside patio area.

Guadalupe River Ranch blends rustic cowboy décor with Hill Country beauty and five-star service.

In total, the ranch can sleep eighty-nine people.

Canoeing and river tubing along the Guadalupe are available, and there's plenty of hiking trails, some quite strenuous (don't forget to drink plenty of water before taking off). Mountain biking, tennis, fly-fishing instruction, and swimming are other popular activities, and let's not forget that "spa" in the ranch's name. How does a Swedish body massage or therapeutic massage sound after riding a horse through the Hill Country? Or a mineral or mud wrap, facial, or special packages?

And about those horses? Many of the ranch's stock are retired racehorses. That doesn't mean you can go galloping pell-mell down the banks of the Guadalupe, but at least you won't be riding Glue Bait.

Hayrides are offered and a few barbecues, and if you're on a family vacation but want a romantic break from the kids, private babysitters can be arranged. Animal feedings are always popular, and the kids probably will enjoy seeing (if not smelling) the ranch's resident pot-bellied pigs, Wilbur and Miss Scarlet.

Guadalupe River Ranch is also perfect for family reunions and weddings, but the entire ranch needs to be rented out for the latter.

All of this has made me hungry, which is one thing you want to be before meals at this ranch.

Breakfast, lunch, and dinner are served at the lodge, inside or on the terrace. The lodge can seat up to 125, and the service is exquisite. The bread is always fresh—the baker's on site—and the ranch raises fresh vegetables and herbs. Dinner is four courses and lunch three. Coffee and drinks are always available in the solarium.

And the food?

"The meal program is definitely the chef's choice," says Patti Massey, the ranch's director of sales and marketing.

Fear not. The chef is Mike McClure, who previously served up fine cuisine at Arizona's Enchantment Resort in Sedona and Loews Ventana Canyon Resort in Tucson.

My dinner included a Caesar salad with a spicy bite and baked chicken breast in mustard sauce, all heavenly—and I don't eat mustard. Other dinner fodder might be duck breast and tenderloin, smoked pork loin, Indian pudding with Texas persimmons, wild onion soup, shrimp bisque, all with Southwestern flavor and an attitude. Dessert is to die for.

There's an extensive wine list, with prices ranging from $16 to $210, but if you're a beer person, several name brands are available as well as bottles from the Yellow Rose microbrewery in San Antonio.

Yep, a stay at Guadalupe River Ranch Resort and Spa is about as pampered as a cowboy/girl can get. Wrecked car aside, my guess is that Olivia de Havilland would gladly return to Guadalupe River Ranch today. And with the first-class service and food, she'd never leave.

Cowboy Savvy

The historic district in downtown Boerne is full of antique and specialty shops, but if you're hungry you might have a hard time grabbing a late lunch. There are some restaurants, but few are serving during that between-lunch-and-supper time. You will find a bunch of fast-food joints near Interstate 10, or you can buy a Pepsi, doughnut, and bagel at the H-E-B grocery, but before you eat, ask yourself:

Why ruin your appetite before sampling the Guadalupe River Ranch's five-star cuisine?

Guadalupe River Ranch Resort and Spa at a Glance

Address: 605 F.M. 474, P.O. Box 877, Boerne, TX 78006

Phone: (800) 460-2005, (830) 537-4837

Fax: (830) 537-5249

E-mail: grranch@gvtc.com

Internet: www.guadaluperiverranch.com

Location: About 8 miles from Boerne off F.M. 474.

Accommodations: 47.

Dining: Breakfast, lunch, dinner.

Rates: $239-$329 double occupancy.

Credit cards: All.

Handicap access: Yes.

Smoking: No.

Pets: No.

Things to do: Two pools. Fishing, hiking, badminton, croquet, jogging, volleyball, basketball, table tennis, and other free activities. Guided canoeing, zip-line rides, trail rides, corral rides, pampering body treatments and massage, guided fishing, river tubing, buggy rides, mountain biking, and hayrides and bonfires are extra.

Season: Open all year.

Lazy Hills Guest Ranch

Ingram

I'm glancing at the map of the Lazy Hills Guest Ranch handed to me after checking in. Shuffleboard, volleyball, swimming pool, bass pond, horse barn . . . yup, this is a dude ranch. But wait a second. What's this on the map just beyond the horse shed/work shop?

Pig barn.

Pig barn?

This might require some investigating. I hike past the horse shed/work shop and see a rawhide-looking pen—definitely not something off a *Green Acres* set—and hear the snorts from a couple of tough-looking, none-too-friendly pigs. They seem a little nervous about my presence. I really don't think much about this until the following morning when I eat my bacon.

Pigs. On a dude ranch. Well, let's not forget that a couple of swine played important roles in Larry McMurtry's Pulitzer Prize- and Spur Award-winning novel *Lonesome Dove*.

The rest of the Lazy Hills is what you would expect at a guest ranch in the Texas Hill Country. Horseback rides ($12 a person per ride, not included in the rates for guests staying less than seven nights; six rides are included for guests staying a week), hayrides, cookouts, campfires, and wildlife viewing. There are twenty-three head of horses and a few cattle. OK, eleven cows, four calves, and one bull when I was there. The rooms may not be Santa Fe's Inn of the Anasazi, but they are certainly cozier than a Wyoming line shack—and the food is exceptional. The staff is mighty friendly.

Like many guest ranches, the Lazy Hills is a family-run operation.

Lazy Hills Guest Ranch: The Past

The 750-acre ranch had been a boys camp when the Steinrucks bought it as an investment in 1959. They bought it sight-unseen while living in Venezuela. Carol Steinruck hated it, daughter-in-law Beth Steinruck says. But don't take Beth's word for it.

"I thought it was the most god-forsaken place I had ever seen," New Jersey native Carol Steinruck says. "We bought it as an investment, and four months later it was an investment of life, and we found out it was a good life. We enjoy serving people."

Carol smiles. "God has his ways," she says.

Lazy Hills Guest Ranch: The Present

At many Western guest ranches, activities are centered on horseback rides, but that's not the case at Lazy Hills. This is a leisurely paced resort. A lot of folks come simply to relax. If you're active-minded, there are more than thirty miles of trails.

"The only thing we really schedule are the three meals," Beth Steinruck says.

Breakfast is served in the dining room from 8 to 9 A.M., lunch is at noon, and supper is at 6 P.M. The schedule varies at mid and low season. Coffee is always ready in the dining room. The food is usually served buffet style, but B&B-style breakfast is the norm during the off season.

The resort is kid-friendly.

"This is an atmosphere for families," Carol Steinruck says. "Children aren't really welcome in a lot of resorts, but we love kids so bring them on."

During peak season, from Memorial Day to Labor Day, several activities are scheduled for children ages two through eight. Activities include singing, arts and crafts, nature walks, and storytelling.

Maybe this goes back to the ranch's days as a boys camp. "We still have a lot of guests who came here as campers and counselors back then," Beth Steinruck says. "They come by and swap stories with us."

The ranch attracts high school groups, seminars, retreats, workshops, even prison groups—er, make that prison guards, who show up for a twelve-day session to learn Spanish. And then there are the hookers.

"They say they'd rather be hookin' than cookin'," Beth Steinruck says.

There's Carol Steinruck's smile again. "I tell people that we have hookers coming in for a seminar and they look at me and say, 'Isn't this a Christian. . . ?' It's rug hooking."

The Round-up Room can seat up to 150 for seminars, retreats, and reunions.

Tennis, volleyball, basketball, shuffleboard, and horseshoes equipment can be checked out in the office. Billiards, table tennis, and foozball can be played in the game room, which also has snack and drink machines. Speaking of drinking, the Lazy Hills has no liquor license so it's BYOB.

For anglers, the ranch has three spring-fed ponds stocked with bass, perch, and catfish. Bait is provided for catfish and cane poles can be bought, but you must bring your own fishing gear. Lures, other bait, and fishing supplies can be bought in Ingram. A license is not required to fish on the ranch.

Guestrooms have twin and queen beds, with electric heat, air conditioning, porches, and bathrooms with showers. Many come

Horses fight off the early morning cold at the lovely Lazy Hills Guest Ranch.

with fireplaces (follow the instructions; you don't want to smoke yourself out of your room). Cribs and highchairs can be requested when making your reservations. There are no telephones or televisions in the rooms, however. After all, this is a getaway. Coin-operated laundry machines are located under the changing rooms at the swimming pool.

Forty years later, Carol Steinruck has no regrets about coming here. She runs the Lazy Hills with the help of her husband, son, and daughter-in-law, along with a staff of about twenty during high season.

The rolling hills, full of deer and other wildlife, have become home—beautiful and pleasant these days instead of "godforsaken."

Says Beth Steinruck: "You could never get her off the place now."

Cowboy Savvy

High season is one thing, but don't overlook a stay at the Lazy Hills during low season. You may not be able to go swimming, but you might have the ranch almost to yourself. And instead of breakfast on the buffet, there's nothing like breakfast made to order. Coffee, juice, meat, eggs, maybe an omelet, and pancakes.

And while supper may not be on the agenda in the winter, the Kerrville-Ingram area features many fine restaurants, from barbecue joints to steak houses and seafood to soda fountains.

Lazy Hills Guest Ranch at a Glance

Address: Henderson Branch Road, P.O. Box G, Ingram, TX 78025

Phone: (800) 880-0632 (reservations only), (830) 367-5600

Fax: (830) 367-5667

E-mail: lhills@ktc.com

Internet: www.lazyhills.com

Location: 2½ miles west of Ingram off State Highway 27 West. Turn right on Henderson Branch Road for 1½ miles.

Accommodations: 25 guest units. Most sleep four comfortably; some will sleep up to six.

Dining: Three meals served daily in season. Out-of-season bed-and-breakfast available.

Rates: Adults ($110 daily, $770 weekly single; $85/$595 double per person; $79/$553 triple per person.) Children: Free daily, $10 crib fee weekly up to 1 year old; Ages 1-8, $35 daily, $245 weekly; 9-11, $40/$280; 12-16, $50/$350.

Credit cards: American Express, Discover, MasterCard, Visa.

Handicap access: No.

Smoking: Yes (but not in dining and game rooms).

Pets: No.

Things to do: Swimming, game room, basketball court,
    volleyball court, tennis court, outdoor shuffleboard, indoor
    shuffleboard, hiking, fishing, hayrides, cookouts, horseback
    riding, gift shop.
Season: Closed Christmas Day.

LH7 Ranch Resort

Bandera

The Suburban slides along the dirt road slick after a Hill
Country rain, but Maudeen Marks saws that wheel as if she took
lessons from Cale Yarborough, straightens the Chevy, and continues on toward the next gate with a hearty laugh.

Now in her eighties and recovering from a broken hip ("These
bones didn't just break," she says. "I broke my hip slipping at 5
A.M. checking on some guests."), Marks has no intention of slow-
ing down. Earlier this morning, she and a young cowboy took the
Suburban pulling a trailer of feed through the ranch. Now she's
giving me a tour of her 1,200-acre LH7 Ranch Resort and intro-
ducing me to her pets.

The pets are more than 200 head of purebred longhorn cattle,
and Marks seems to know each bull, cow, and steer by name.
This isn't your ordinary herd, though. The LH7 cattle have been
blood-typed for purity and chosen for research at Texas A&M
University.

"My cattle are not for fun," she says. "My cattle are for real
and are my purpose."

That's all part of the LH7 legacy.

LH7 Ranch Resort: The Past

Emil Henry Marks was born on October 25, 1881, the son of German immigrants. He became a top cowboy on several ranches in southeastern Texas, but he knew he wanted to be a rancher. He registered his LH7 brand in Harris County in 1898. He married Maud May Smith in 1907 and bought 63 acres in Addicks and a small house from an old widow, and, with a few head of cattle, the LH7 Ranch was born.

Ten years later Marks sold his small ranch and bought a section of grasslands in Barker. On April 2, 1918, Maud Marks gave birth to her fourth child, Maudeen Martha.

By the 1920s the Texas longhorns had almost been bred out of extinction, and E.H. Marks wanted to preserve the herd. A silent movie, *North of 36*, was filmed on a neighboring ranch, and several of Marks's longhorns served as "extras" in the Western. Hollywood aside, Marks strove to raise pure longhorns and he became well known throughout the state for his goal. J. Frank Dobie's outstanding book *The Longhorns* features photographs of some LH7 cattle.

E.H. Marks died in 1969, and Maud died less than a year later. Maudeen was left with the Barker house and a few head of cattle, and with help from her brother Travis she continued her father's legacy by breeding registered longhorns.

Tired of Houston's urban sprawl, Maudeen decided to move the LH7. She bought a ranch in Bandera in 1982 "because there was plenty of room and we're off the road."

The ranch came with ten cottages, however, and Maudeen decided it was perfect for guests.

"I don't call myself a dude ranch," Maudeen says. "I'm a real ranch with guest accommodations."

LH7 Ranch Resort: The Present

The clean stone cottages include a full kitchen, which is important to note because the LH7 offers no set meals, although the ranch can cater for groups of at least twenty. Most cottages have two double beds and a couch that can convert into a single bed, while some have bunk beds. All have heating and air conditioning and a full-size refrigerator. Fishing and swimming are included in the rates, but horseback riding is extra. Belle Meeks is the wrangler but has only six horses. "We're a small operation," she says. She offers half-hour, one-, and two-hour trail rides on gentle horses for those eight years old and up, and pony rides for younger children. Discounts are offered for overnight guests at the LH7.

The ranch also has eighteen RV sites and several campsites for tents. The lodge can be rented for exclusive use, and so can the ranch.

Bird watching and fishing are popular pastimes, but perhaps the best way to spend your time at the LH7 is to take a ranch tour. Individual and group tours as well as pasture hayrides are offered. Of course, you don't have to tour the pastures to see the longhorns. Several steers roam around the grounds, and retired bull Coronado is a popular subject of photographers. "That's not someone knocking on your door at 2 A.M.," Belle Meeks says. "That's a longhorn. The cattle are a fixture here. They're not meat, they're not milk. They're tradition and heritage."

And few people know longhorns better than Maudeen Marks.

"A bull's horns sit back and forward for defense," she explains. "When male calves are castrated at six or eight months old, it changes the hormones and thus changes the shape of the steer's horns."

Marks's informative tours last about two hours. "We have thirteen pastures, and we'll go through at least six or seven, past Indian mounds, and Blue Hole on the Medina River. We're very flexible."

She enjoys the tours. "We have really nice people who come here." Mostly, Maudeen Marks enjoys her "pets," and ranching, which she has done all of her life.

"The cowboy business is the Western life," she says.

Purebred longhorn cattle are the real stars at the LH7 Ranch Resort.

Cowboy Savvy

For special guests, Belle Meeks will be pleased to offer you a parting gift, donated by the LH7's own Coronado. The present, in a zip-lock bag, comes complete with a label so you can show it off to your friends or use it as fertilizer in your garden back home.

"Genuine Texas Bull-..." Well, you get the idea.

LH7 Ranch Resort at a Glance

Address: P.O. Box 1474, Bandera, TX 78003

Phone: (830) 796-4314

Fax: N/A

E-mail: N/A

Internet: N/A

Location: 3½ miles from Bandera off F.M. 3240 at Montague Ranch Estates.

Accommodations: 10 guest cottages. Plus 18 RV hookups and tent sites.

Dining: None except by special arrangement. Full kitchens provided in cottages.

Rates: Cottages: $57.50-$65 double occupancy daily (weekly and 3-day packages available). RV Hookups $10 daily double occupancy, $60 weekly. Camping: $5 per person daily, $30 weekly.

Credit cards: None.

Handicap access: No.

Smoking: Yes.

Pets: No.

Things to do: Ranch tours, fishing (catch-and-release except for catfish), hiking, birding, horseback riding (not included in price), canoeing, hayrides by request.

Season: Open all year.

Mayan Dude Ranch

Bandera

To call the Mayan Dude Ranch a family operation is a whopper of an understatement. Don and Judy Hicks own the guest ranch that is just about as close to the actual town of Bandera as you can get. Helping out are eleven of the Hicks's children and a couple of their spouses.

With a staff of twenty-six, including three-and-a-half cooks, you can bet your boots that you'll be pampered and entertained on this 345-acre ranch horseshoed by the Medina River. One thing's for certain: The Hicks family certainly knows how to run a guest ranch. Yup, they're about as Texan as you can get.

Only they're from Wisconsin.

Mayan Dude Ranch: The Past

The ranch began as a Girl Scout camp—you can still see the Scout insignia in the fireplace in the Round Up Room, son Tim Hicks points out—in the early 1930s.

Dr. J.R. Brinkley of Del Rio and Rose Dawn of San Antonio took over the ranch after the Girl Scouts left. Doc Brinkley might be best known for his "rejuvenation" surgery, which required implanting goat glands in men's prostates for the added vigor and no more impotence. I've never met anyone who admitted to having the surgery or was willing to testify that it worked.

Anyway, Bill Morse of Houston bought the ranch in the early 1950s, and the Mayan became a dude ranch. In 1951 E.A. and Grace Hicks bought the ranch. Don Hicks came down after graduating from Notre Dame and started running the ranch in 1952.

But what about the name Mayan?

"The Mayan was the name that was there," daughter Shea Butler says, "and we decided to keep it."

Adds Tim Hicks: "I wish it had something to do with the Mayan Indians, but it doesn't." Some tourists think it's named after rodeo star and Western personality Larry Mahan.

Nope. Check the spelling, folks.

Of course, Larry Mahan would feel mighty comfortable in his boots at this ranch. In fact, the Mayan is probably one of the most popular ranches in all of Bandera, the self-claimed "Cowboy Capital of the World."

Mayan Dude Ranch: The Present

First, let's take a look at the accommodations. The Mayan has thirty-eight rock cottages with one, two, and three bedrooms, some with fireplaces, all well decorated, kind of John Wayne meets Martha Stewart. There are also thirty hotel/motel-type rooms, with a king-size bed and bath adjoining with two double beds and a bath.

Nestled among the heavily wooded hills, these cottages and rooms offer solitude, even wildlife viewing, the perfect places to unwind after a day of playing cowboy.

You definitely get more than "three hots and a cot" at the Mayan Dude Ranch.

Oh, and if you happen to wake up in the middle of the night to a terrifying scream, fear not. It's only a peacock.

Your day begins with the 7:30 A.M. wake-up call and a newsletter explaining the day's events. How do you have a wake-up call when there are no phones in the room? They just knock on your door.

Need an example of a day at the Mayan?

Cowboy breakfast: Horses depart at 8:45 A.M. and the hay wagon, if you don't want to fork a saddle before eating, at 9 A.M., with grub prepared on the trail.... Inside breakfast (if you don't want to ride a horse or wagon to eat): 7:30-10 A.M.... Later morning horse ride: 10:30 A.M.... Complimentary draft beer, wine, and sodas at the saloon: 11 A.M. to 7 P.M. (Kids, by the way, aren't allowed in the saloon.)... Lunch in the dining room: 12:15-12:45 P.M.... Afternoon horse ride: 3 P.M.... Hayride: 5 P.M.... Snacks inside the saloon: 5:45 P.M.... Steaks and entertainment in the dining room: 7 P.M.... Karaoke inside the saloon: 8:30 P.M.

That's a full day.

The cowboy breakfast, served hot on the trail, includes eggs, grits, hash browns, bacon, homemade link sausage, biscuits, and daily specials. The Mayan is well known for its grub: mesquite-cooked steaks, brisket, pork, ribs, chicken, sausage, turkey, Mexican fare, even a Cornish game hen or Judy Hicks's zucchini pancakes.

"Beans and weenies," Tim Hicks says. "That's definitely not us."

Breakfast and lunch are usually served buffet style.

A stay at the Mayan includes two horseback rides daily, but remember the rules: Maximum weight is 240 pounds. Riders must be at least six years old. No riding double. Pregnant women not allowed on walking rides without a doctor's written permission. All rides are single-file and guided, usually lasting about an hour, either into the hills or along the Medina River.

Oh, in June, July, and August, the horses take Sundays off.

This is definitely a dude ranch. The Mayan runs about fifty horses, including draft animals to pull the hay wagon, and only one cow, named Norman Vincent Veal.

Besides ridin' and eatin', there are plenty of things to do. The Mayan has a swimming pool as well as a hot tub and volleyball, basketball, and tennis courts. Several nature trails are perfect for hiking, and you can tube down the Medina—if the river's deep enough. Remember, South Texas is prone to drought, so don't count on a tubing vacation. Inner tubes are available for rent in town. Fishing for catfish, bass, and perch is also permitted on the river.

If it rains?

Well, that's what the Hicks gang is here for. You might not be able to hit the trail on a horse or enjoy a steak fry at the ranch's ghost town, but the staff will come up with a variety of games. Maybe they'll schedule a sing-a-long, or teach you how to do the Texas Two-Step or Cotton-Eyed Joe. Shucks, there's always some form of entertainment before, during, and after the evening meal.

"Sometimes," Shea Butler says, "I think we have as much fun as the guests."

Cowboy Savvy

Since we're in Bandera, now's a good time to mention the Frontier Times Museum. The museum, at 506 13th St., includes 40,000 artifacts including tools, saddles, clothes, telephones, schoolbooks, firearms, prehistoric items, and an old telephone switchboard.

The museum began as historian and newspaper journalist J. Marvin Hunter Senior's collection. Hunter, editor of *Frontier Times* magazine and the massive chronicle of Texas cowboys, *The Trail Drivers of Texas*, started the museum in 1921 in a small room. When his collection became too big for the room, he printed a book and raised $1,000 to build a new building in 1933.

Today, the museum attracts about 12,000 people each year. It is open 10 A.M. to 4:30 P.M. Monday through Saturday and 1-4:30 P.M. Sunday. Admission is $2 for adults, 25 cents for children 6-18, and free for teachers, school groups, and children under six.

Mayan Dude Ranch at a Glance

Address: P.O. Box 577, Bandera, TX 78003

Phone: (830) 796-3312, (830) 460-3036

Fax: (830) 796-8205

E-mail: mayan@express-news.net

Internet: www.mayanranch.com

Location: 1½ miles outside of Bandera.

Accommodations: 68 rooms: 38 rock cottages with 1, 2, and 3 bedrooms; some with fireplaces; 30 hotel/motel accommodations with 1 king and bath adjoining 2 double & bath.

Dining: All meals included. Cowboy breakfast, breakfast buffet, lunch buffet, cookouts.

Rates: Adults $120 per day. Age 13-17, $80. Age 12 and under $55. Plus 10 percent gratuity and state tax.

Credit cards: All.

Handicap access: Yes.

Smoking: Yes.

Pets: No.

Things to do: Horseback riding, swimming, hot tub, hiking, fishing, volleyball, basketball, tennis, summer rodeos, horseshoe and washer pitching, shuffleboard, children's programs, bingo, wildlife viewing, country-western dance lessons, trick roping, peacock feather hunting, fossil and arrowhead hunting.

Season: Open all year.

Prude Ranch

Fort Davis

There's a Girl Scout camp south of here at Mitre Peak and a Boy Scout camp north of here near Toyahvale. Yet that hasn't stopped Prude Ranch from holding a successful youth camp for boys and girls each summer, a tradition that dates to 1951.

Don't think Prude Ranch is just for kids, though. As cowhand Bounce McFerran points out: "We do it all. We don't short on nobody."

There are star parties (the ranch is only fifteen minutes from the McDonald Observatory), tennis courts, an indoor swimming pool, birding and hiking trails. Of course, since this is a dude ranch, you can arrange horseback rides ($15 an hour; $25 for two hours; overnight and half-day excursions can be arranged in advance) and a roping pen. Stalls can be rented if you want to bring your own horse. There's even a weeklong excursion to Mexico's Copper Canyon available.

Including leased land, Prude Ranch has about 5,000 acres and runs 400 head of cattle. This isn't just a dude ranch, mind you. It's still a working cattle operation, and it has been for more than a hundred years.

Prude Ranch: The Past

In the 1890s "Grandma" Ora Prude lit a shuck for West Texas and traveled by covered wagon from Indiana to the Davis Mountains. Brothers John and Claiborne Prude, with sons John C. and Andrew, drove 3,000 cattle from McCulloch County to West Texas.

Andrew G. Prude married Ora in 1896 and established Prude Ranch along Limpia Creek in the Davis Mountains in 1897. The Prudes started out in a log cabin but moved into a frame house in 1900. The "Big House," a two-story adobe, was completed in 1911. The Prudes prospered until the cattle market collapsed and a terrible drought struck West Texas after World War I. By 1920 the Prude Ranch encompassed forty sections, or 25,600 acres.

In 1922, in an effort to help make ends meet, the Prudes began accepting paying guests. John G. "Big Spurs" Prude, the second generation, became involved, and his son, John Robert Prude, and daughter-in-law, Betty, started the youth program. The Prudes have been at it ever since. Well in his nineties, "Big

Spurs" Prude still oversees the working ranch operation, while John Robert and Betty handle the "dude" work.

Prude Ranch: The Present

The ranch has several accommodations, from guest lodges (holding up to four people) to bunkhouses (with rooms capable of holding from eight to twenty), and two campgrounds with forty full hookups. This isn't posh, but it's down-home and comfortable, and the Prudes go out of their way to hire friendly and knowledgeable cowboys who are great with children.

Dining is served cafeteria style. The dining room serves breakfast daily ($5.50 and up), but lunch ($6 and up) and dinner ($7.95 and up) are available only when the ranch has twenty or more registered guests. The hall can seat up to 200 people. If more guests are at the ranch, you'll be fed in shifts.

Good, old-fashioned hoe-downs are sometimes scheduled, complete with chuck wagon, cowboy poets, western music, and the like.

Prude Ranch might be best known for its work with children between ages 7 and 15. There are one- and two-week sessions offered each summer. Sessions are divided into age groups (7-9, 10-11, 12-13, 14-15). Scouts can earn merit badges. The ranch has also offered youth equestrian programs for troubled, blind, and those with Down syndrome. Younger kids can hit a petting zoo. Tuition runs from $495 to $550 for one-week classes and $965 to $995 for two-week classes. The camp staff includes certified teachers and college students. Two registered nurses are on duty at all times, and the camp doctor has an office in Fort Davis.

Cowboy Savvy

Stables, trails, and horse apples are commonplace for a dude ranch, but Prude Ranch also takes its star-gazing seriously. And well it should. The Davis Mountains, with clear skies and an elevation of 5,500 feet, have long attracted amateur and professional

Few ranches can match the rugged beauty of the Davis Mountains at Prude Ranch.

astronomers. Prude Ranch has a star pad for those who enjoy the night skies. Red porch lights and covered windows in occupied rooms are further proof that the ranch is serious about cutting down on light pollution.

Prude Ranch at a Glance

Address: P.O. Box 1431, Fort Davis, TX 79734

Phone: (800) 458-6232, (915) 426-3202

Fax: (915) 426-3502

E-mail: prude@overland.net

Internet: www.prude-ranch.com

Location: 6 miles northwest of Fort Davis on Highway 118.

Accommodations: 42 rooms, 6 bunkhouses that can sleep up to 200, plus two RV campgrounds.

Dining: Cafeteria-style restaurant. Hours vary depending on business.

Rates: Rooms $65 singles, $75 doubles. Bunkhouses $49 singles, $58 doubles, plus $10 per extra person. Group discounts available.

Credit cards: American Express, Discover, MasterCard, Visa.

Handicap access: One room.

Smoking: No.

Pets: No.

Things to do: Trail rides, hiking and birding trails, indoor swimming pool, tennis courts, gift shop. One- and two-week summer camps are offered for boys and girls during the summer.

Season: Open all year.

Rough Creek Lodge Executive Retreat and Resort

Glen Rose

Paul Boccafogli, general manager of Rough Creek Lodge, praises his staff of approximately ninety to a hundred employees at this upscale resort about ninety minutes southwest of Dallas-Fort Worth.

"We get compliments on the staff all the time," he says. "We have a very good group of employees. It's like a family, which is what I always wanted. Most of the staff didn't know anything about five-star quality service, but they learned quickly. There's a lot of training—it's part of our daily activity [the resort even offers a student-internship program]—but the people here are very, very friendly. It's casual, but very professional."

You'll get no argument here.

The staffers here, many of them locals from Glen Rose and nearby Cleburne and Stephenville, know that you can have the best location, rooms, and food around (and Rough Creek is close to the top on all accounts), but if you don't have first-class service, the guests won't be coming back.

So Rough Creek Lodge strives to provide a country-sophisticated-service attitude to offer, in Boccafogli's words, "a very comfortable, friendly, service-oriented five-star experience."

And you definitely get that—not to mention remarkable cuisine—whether you come to the resort as part of an executive retreat, to hunt upland game birds, or simply to get out of the city for a remarkable, unforgettable weekend getaway.

All of which holds true to owner John Q. Adams Sr.'s original idea.

Rough Creek Lodge: The Past

A retired pharmaceuticals industry executive, Adams saw the need to build a lodge that offered a place for corporate retreats and hunting. He bought 11,140 acres in the rolling hills of the Chalk Mountain Ranch in the early 1990s. The problem was that, according to studies, hunting operations fared well for five months but performed poorly the rest of the year.

But if you also offered exceptional meeting facilities, luxury, great food, and seclusion, you could fill a void and attract customers when hunting isn't allowed.

"This was clearly his vision from the beginning," Boccafogli says. "What's unique about this is that we offer service to three groups: the transient; the individual traveler; and the conferences, where most of them stay two to four days and are here for retreats, strategy or planning sessions, team building, or incentives, meaning they got here as a prize. The third aspect is hunting. Mr. Adams's vision was unique because of the hunting component."

Designed by Larry Speck, the Lodge was constructed of native limestone, with the interior featuring wrought iron, a forty-foot limestone fireplace, sixty-foot ceilings, and an upscale Texas decor, with big, cozy chairs and leather sofas.

The price tag for design, development, and training hit $25 million. Rough Creek Lodge opened on January 20, 1998, and became an immediate hit.

Rough Creek Lodge: The Present

Guestrooms come with oversize beds and baths, complete with deep tubs and separate showers. Private balconies, including rocking chairs, offer a view of the resort's lake. Deluxe guestrooms ($325 single or double occupancy) come with one king or two European single beds. Suites include the Executive ($525), with a large sitting area; the One-Bedroom ($725), with a living room area and dining table for four; and the 1,300-square-foot George Bush Presidential ($1,200), complete with a large living area and half-bath and a dining area for eight. Each room has a satellite television and dual telephone lines for modem and phone use. A nightly turn-down service is provided, and room service is available 24 hours a day.

The resort includes 63 ponds, 64.3 miles of ranch road, and 73.2 miles of fences.

A sauna and heated outdoor pool are on the site, along with a fitness center. Feel free to use the telescope, and if you enjoy catch-and-release fishing, fly-fishing and standard fishing equipment and bass boats can be provided. Wildlife tours are offered, and guests can play tennis (rackets and balls are available), basketball, table tennis, horseshoes, and croquet, not to mention mountain biking, archery, and five-stand shooting competition. There's also a rifle range. Shooting instruction is offered.

For additional fees, Rough Creek offers four-hour guided fishing trips (maximum of two guests per guide, $100 for guide) and two-hour sporting-clay rounds (100 targets, $40 per round with two-guest minimum).

Worn out from all of that? Well, schedule an hour-long (or longer) massage ($75-$112), a facial ($60), pedicure ($60), or manicure ($40).

Of course, one of the main attractions at Rough Creek is the bird hunting. The resort remains a working cattle ranch, but 3,000 acres are used solely as a hunting preserve. It's strictly bird hunting here, for pheasant, quail, Hungarian partridge, and chukar. Hunting season runs from October to March, and bird outings include a warm-up shoot, a truck, guide, bird dogs, processing, and packaging. Beretta 686 Onyx over-and-under shotguns are provided, along with hunting jackets, vests, and hats. There's no bag limit or per-bird charge.

Packages offered include half-day, 24-hour (two hunts over two days), businessman's (Sunday and Monday only), three-day executive (four hunts over three days), and even "Birds & Birdies," which is one day of hunting and another day of golf.

In charge of the hunting and other recreation activities is Wayne "W.C." Collins, hired as director of wildlife and recreation services in 1999. Before arriving at Rough Creek, Collins spent two years managing hunting camps in South Texas and Mexico and served as the day-to-day operations manager of the upscale Hawkeye Hunting Club for six years.

"Safety is our first concern," Boccafogli says, "and then have fun—and you can do both."

If hunting isn't your bag, the resort offers packages for weddings, special events, and meetings. For the corporate minded, you'll find four meeting rooms, holding sixteen to a hundred people, in the Lodge. The Texas Room has 760 square feet, the Longhorn 840, Chalk Mountain I 940, and Chalk Mountain II 760. The Chalk Mountain rooms can be turned into one 1,700-square-foot room that can seat 100 theater-style. The meeting rooms can use built-in rear projection screens, high resolution

Rough Creek Lodge is a hunting lodge, corporate retreat, and upscale romantic getaway all rolled into one.

video/data projector, 35mm slide projector, overhead projector, wireless microphone, and a full sound system, all controlled by wireless remote.

Finally, there's the food, which has been praised in the Texas media, including the *Fort Worth Star-Telegram*, to the national media, including *American Way*, *Fortune*, *Robb Report*, and *Veranda* magazines.

The menu varies and is always a treat, from a spicy seafood gumbo to sherry maple glazed quail or sweet potato soup to wild-flower honey-dipped French toast. There's also an extensive wine list. With food and service like this, why would you ever leave the dining room?

This delectable experience is the product of Gerard Thompson, hired as executive chef and food and beverage director in 1997—before the Lodge opened for business. Thompson's credentials are flawless. He was executive chef of the Stonehouse restaurant at San Ysidro Ranch in Santa Barbara, California, for six years, was sous chef at Houston's Remington Hotel, and also worked at Houston's Hyatt Regency and San Antonio's Crockett Hotel.

So Thompson makes sure you won't leave Rough Creek Lodge hungry, and the rest of the staff will make sure you definitely won't forget your experience.

Cowboy Savvy

Worth checking out in the Lodge is the Gene Autry boot on display, complete with spur and spur strap. The boot was made by Cosimo Lucchese. The silver and gold spur is the product of Marlin Spurgeon, and the leather strap was tooled by Tad S. Mizwa, creating a unique piece of Western history in the style of the noted Edward Bohlin.

And although you won't find boots and spurs for sale, the Lodge's gift shop offers shirts, caps, and other apparel.

Rough Creek Lodge at a Glance

Address: P.O. Box 2400, Glen Rose, TX 76043

Phone: (800) 864-4705, (254) 965-3700

Fax: (254) 918-2570

E-mail: reservations@roughcreek.com

Internet: www.roughcreek.com

Location: 16 miles southwest of Glen Rose off Highway 67 on County Road 2013.

Accommodations: 39 guestrooms and suites.

Dining: Breakfast, lunch, dinner.

Rates: $325-$1,200 daily.

Credit cards: All.

Handicap access: Yes.

Smoking: Yes.

Pets: Yes.

Things to do: Game-bird hunting (October to March), sporting clays, tennis, basketball, croquet, softball, archery, rifle range, fly-fishing and shooting instruction, biking, catch-and-release fishing, sauna and outdoor heated pool, hiking. Gift shop and meeting rooms on site.

Season: Open all year.

Running-R Guest Ranch

Bandera

At only 227 acres, the Running-R Guest Ranch is small compared to some of the sprawling ranches that accept paying guests throughout the West. Of course, few of those massive ranches bump up against a 5,500-acre preserve filled with oak and cedar, deer, rabbits, coyotes, and even mountain lions.

So with access to the Hill Country State Natural Area (the park's entry fee is $3 daily per person over 12 years old), the Running-R can offer more than forty miles of trails for horseback rides, some of them pretty challenging.

"The main difference between us and other guest ranches is the horseback riding," owner Iris Kirchner says.

In addition to meals and other ranch activities, the rates include two hours of horseback riding per day. "Most people choose two-hour rides, but you can also do riding into one piece or one- to five- or six-hour rides," Kirchner says.

There's no double-riding, and you have to be six or older to ride. Additional rides are $13 per hour, and riding lessons are offered at $30 an hour. Horseback rides ($14-$80 per person, plus park entrance fee) are also available for visitors who aren't spending the night, but you need to make reservations at least one day in advance.

The ranch runs about thirty-five head of horses.

Running-R Guest Ranch: The Past

The Running-R used to be a working ranch before Iris Kirchner and her husband, Ralph, entered the scene. Charles "Doo" Robbins had worked on various dude ranches, including the nearby Dixie Dude Ranch, and was looking for partners to help him start his own guest ranch. The Kirchners were Texas guest ranch veterans.

"The first time we came to Bandera was as tourists" in the late 1980s, Iris Kirchner says. "We got tired of traveling around, and somebody told us about the guest ranches and horseback riding around Bandera. That would be it, we thought, so we came to Bandera, liked it, and came back for two weeks. That went on for three years, twice a year."

Oh, did I mention the Kirchners were living in Germany at the time?

Maybe it's cheaper to live in Texas and run a guest ranch than to travel overseas twice a year and pay to stay.

Anyway, the Kirchners and Robbins went into business together in the early 1990s, and the Running-R suddenly grew. "We really more or less fell into it," Iris says. "We got a lot of requests, first about accommodations, then about offering meals."

Today, the Running-R is a bona fide guest ranch, and the Kirchners and Robbins are the perfect hosts.

Running-R Guest Ranch: The Present

"Everything looks old but is really pretty new," Iris says.

That goes from the corrals to the fourteen cabins. Each cabin has a private bathroom, heating and air conditioning, refrigerator, and porch. Cabins can sleep up to four people, and a bunkhouse can accommodate up to six. And while many guest ranches offer spartan sleeping quarters and/or meals that aren't exactly five-star quality, you definitely get more than three hots and a cot at the Running-R.

"Everybody loves the food," Iris says. "There's nothing coming out of a can."

Home-cooked meals are served buffet-style in the Round-up room. The cabins may look rough on the outside, but inside they are spacious, clean, and cozy with a rustic decor. In fact, everything about the ranch looks authentic.

Well, maybe not the swimming pool.

"I didn't want to put a swimming pool in—they're nothing but trouble," Doo Robbins says, "but the first thing folks ask when they call is, 'Do you have a swimming pool?' so...."

The staff includes three cooks and at least four wranglers, and there are twenty-one longhorn cattle ready to show off. For an added bonus, maybe Doo will call the longhorns for you. It's definitely nothing like Eddie Arnold singing "Cattle Call."

If you're not into horseback riding (or swimming), other ranch activities include hayrides, horseshoes, table tennis, and occasional barbecues, breakfast rides, and campfires.

The Kirchners and Robbins definitely know how to run a guest ranch. They learned some important lessons as ranch guests and a ranch hand, respectively.

"When we were staying at a guest ranch, we expected to be treated nice," Iris says.

Make no mistake about it. Guests are treated "nice" at the Running-R.

Charles "Doo" Robbins successfully calls a longhorn to the fence at the Running-R Guest Ranch.

Cowboy Savvy

My first realization of how big Texas guest ranches are overseas probably came when I picked up a magazine at the X Bar

Ranch in Eldorado. The magazine was in German. While visiting the Running-R, Iris Kirchner took a phone call and began speaking German. The one guest staying at the Running-R while I was there was German. Etain Nugent, the ranch's head wrangler, came from Ireland.

"I think people overseas have discovered that winters in Texas aren't all that bad," Doo Robbins says. "What may be cold to us is light-sweater weather to them. Things that are Western are huge in Germany and Italy, and it's getting that way in Austria. Switzerland has also taken to it."

Guest ranches also attract visitors from the Northeast and Midwest. Among Texas cities, San Antonio (only 55 miles from Bandera) and Houston send a lot of visitors to dude ranches. Houston seems to be the big winner.

"We have a saying here," Doo Robbins says with a smile. "The only things that keep Bandera green are Houston and rain."

Running-R Guest Ranch at a Glance

Address: 9059 Bandera Creek Road, Bandera, TX 78003

Phone: (830) 796-3984

Fax: (830) 796-8189

E-mail: runningr@texas.net

Internet: www.rrranch.com

Location: 9.5 miles southwest of Bandera off Ranch Road 1077 next to Hill Country State Natural Area.

Accommodations: 14 cabins, each sleeps up to four people, bunkhouse up to six. All with private bathrooms, air conditioning/heating, refrigerator, and porch.

Dining: Three meals per day served in Round-up Room.

Rates: Rates include three meals per day, 2 hours of horseback riding per day, and all other activities. Minimum stay: Two nights. Adult rates: $80-$95 daily, $540-$635 weekly. Children: $45-$55/$290-$360.

Credit cards: Discover, MasterCard, Visa.

Handicap access: No.

Smoking: Yes.

Pets: No.

Things to do: Horseback rides (1-5 hours), swimming pool, horseshoe pitching, hayrides, barbecues, cowboy breakfasts, table tennis, pool table. Riding lessons available. Tubing, canoeing, seasonal rodeos, and golfing nearby.

Season: Open all year. High season March-October.

Twin Elm Guest Ranch

Bandera

A deer that thinks it's a dog comes up to owner Charlsie Browne as she's showing me around Twin Elm Guest Ranch. The deer wants to be petted, and the dogs roaming around this Bandera ranch on the Medina River ignore the "pet."

This isn't exactly what you would call wildlife. But the rest of the ranch looks truly authentic, from the corrals to the cabins to the chuck wagon. If the ranch looks like it has been here for a while, it has. The main house was built in 1935 and the dining room in 1939.

"It's a little too rustic for some people," Browne says, "but you make friends up here and you keep them, and that's nice."

Browne should know. Although she has been owner of this roughly 200-acre ranch only since the late 1990s, she's a Twin Elm veteran.

Twin Elm Guest Ranch: The Past

The original ranch was built in 1935 as a working stock ranch in the Bandera Hills. Water was no problem what with Indian

Creek and the spring-fed Medina River flowing through the rolling, tree-thick hills.

In 1939 the family-run ranch turned toward the hospitality business, and it has stayed that way through various owners ever since then. Charlsie Browne, born and raised in Houston, showed up for the first time in 1966, when her parents left her here for two weeks at a girls camp.

"I came back every year until I was too old to attend camp," Browne says, "and then they hired me as a counselor."

By the early 1990s, Charlsie wanted to buy the ranch. Not any dude ranch, though, just the Twin Elm. "I never even considered any other ranch," she says.

It took four years for her to convince the owners to sell, but the family finally agreed, and Browne became a bona fide guest ranch owner.

"It's what I really wanted to do," she says. "I had no experience in dude ranches except what I did as a camper and then as a counselor. I sold everything I have and absolutely love it."

Twin Elm Guest Ranch: The Present

As owner, Browne decided to change what she didn't like about the ranch as a guest. The first thing to go were the beds. "If you don't get a good night's rest, you're not going to have any fun," she says. So the twenty-one guestrooms these days have comfy beds covered with colorful quilts.

Most rooms have private baths, some have bunk beds, and others have two double beds or a double and a twin. The lodge has a screened-in porch, while the cabins have open porches. While all rooms are air-conditioned, you will not find a television or telephone unless you head to the recreation room.

A typical day at the Twin Elm begins with not your typical wake-up call. "Cattle Call" sounds out on the jukebox to let you know it's time to get dressed and get ready for breakfast.

The Twin Elm Guest Ranch may be a little too rustic for some, but most visitors love it.

Speaking of breakfast, rates include three meals a day (except there's no supper Sunday night), served buffet style in the dining hall or outside off the chuck wagon.

"Mealtime is the only thing cut in stone around here," Browne says. "Horseback riding is pretty much flexible."

Most of those trail rides cross the clear waters of the river or creek, but if you're not into riding horses, maybe a trip down the Medina in a tube is more to your way of liking to kill a summer afternoon. The Twin Elm provides both tubes and transportation.

The ranch also has a swimming pool and offers horseshoes and washer tournaments, along with marshmallow roasts and cowboy singing. A recreation room includes billiard and Ping-Pong tables, television, videocassette recorder, and plenty of books and videos.

Most stays require a minimum of three nights, although two-night reservations are accepted on some days. The ranch doesn't sell alcohol, and hourly horseback riding is offered for non-guests by reservation. You can also rent out the entire ranch for reunions, weddings, and parties.

Twin Elm still attracts various youth groups, including senior classes, school and youth clubs, church groups, and Boy and Girl Scouts. If you can't stay overnight, day trips are options for groups of twenty or more. A 9:30 A.M.-to-4 P.M. plan, at $30 a person, includes a barbecue lunch and horseback riding, plus other ranch activities. A 10 A.M.-to-7 P.M. plan, at $40 a person, features lunch and horseback riding plus a hayride and wiener roast with chili.

The ranch is small, with a summer staff of about nine and about twenty-five head of horses, and it's definitely children-friendly. After all, Charlsie Browne hasn't forgotten how much fun she had here as a kid.

"Parents can sit on the front porches and know their kids aren't going to get in any trouble," Browne says. "The kids run themselves silly, and we always have something going on for the kids. Parents always like it if you can wear the kids out."

Cowboy Savvy

One highlight of a summer stay at Twin Elm Guest Ranch is the Friday night rodeo, free for overnight guests. The rodeo begins with the Star Spangled Grand Entry, followed by plenty of bull riding, steer riding, roping, and barrel racing. The staff increases to about thirty people on rodeo night.

Of course, this being the "Cowboy Capital of the World," it's a pretty good bet that Bandera has a lot of rodeos throughout the summer. The biggest is the Cowboy Capital Rodeo Association's event at Mansfield Park, an honest-to-goodness Professional Rodeo Cowboys Association contest held during Memorial Day weekend. Other rodeos include the Oxbow Arena's Saturday night series, the Ranch Rodeo at Mansfield Park on Labor Day weekend, and a Tuesday night series at Mansfield Park.

Twin Elm Guest Ranch at a Glance

Address: F.M. 470 at Highway 16, P.O. Box 117, Bandera, TX
78003

Phone: (888) 567-3049, (830) 796-3628

Fax: N/A.

E-mail: N/A.

Internet: www.twinelmranch.com

Location: Off F.M. 470 just south of State Highway 16 in
Bandera.

Accommodations: 21 rooms.

Dining: 3 meals daily included.

Rates: $90 per adult per night, $60 ages 13-17, $50 ages 3-12.

Credit cards: American Express, MasterCard, Visa.

Handicap access: No.

Smoking: Yes.

Pets: No.

Things to do: Horseback riding, river tubing, swimming pool,
summer rodeos, game room, horseshoes, fossil hunting.

Season: Open all year.

X Bar Ranch

Eldorado

Stan Meador sometimes finds it a little bit hard trying to
explain exactly what the X Bar Ranch is.

"In the beginning," he says, "we kinda had an identity crisis."

That's because in one sense, the X Bar Ranch is part B&B
(the food's Continental, but the ranch in Schleicher County is
definitely isolated). But this is also a working ranch in west-cen-

tral Texas, and it certainly isn't a dude ranch. "We try to market ourselves away from Bandera," Meador says, referring to the Hill Country's "Cowboy Capital of the World" and its bevy of dude ranches.

So the Meador family finally opted to call the X Bar a Working Guest Ranch.

"But even that wasn't exactly what we wanted," Meador says. "People have this preconceived idea of coming here and riding horseback and rounding up cattle, and we're so far from there it's not even funny."

Well, not exactly. The Meadors work cattle on their 7,100-acre spread where the Hill Country meets the Edwards Plateau. They work goats and sheep, too—you can even spot a few emus—and guests can help out doing ranch work if they feel up to it, be it lambing, calving, branding, shearing sheep, or mending fence.

"One thing we decided early was that we won't create work simply for our guests," Meador says. "We aren't Bandera, where you can have two-week stays and play city slicker. But we go to great lengths for people to try to understand what they're getting before they come out here."

What they're getting, naturally, is a working ranch that accepts paying guests.

X Bar Ranch: The Past

C.L. "Uncle Dink" Meador probably never envisioned this when he first arrived in Eldorado back in 1903. The Schleicher County seat (actually, the only community in the county) was established in 1895. It was a pretty good stopping point for travelers because it had water. Today, Eldorado is a pretty good stopping point because it's at the junction of U.S. Highways 190 and 277, and it's still the only community in Schleicher County.

"Uncle Dink" came from Lampasas with wife Mattie and four sons, C.L. Junior, Frank, Clyde, and Cecil. They made camp in town under a big mesquite, and "Uncle Dink" began buying land in the area. The Meadors established themselves as a ranching family, and subsequent generations have continued the legacy.

C.L. Meador Junior's second son, Ed, took over ranch operations after World War II. Ed remains active in the ranch today, with help from son Lynn and grandsons Stan and Chris.

The bunkhouses started out as part of a hunting lease operation in 1996. That didn't really work out, and when the Meadors tried to figure out what they could now do with those bunkhouses, they decided to take a crack at the hospitality business. In 1997 the X Bar Ranch began accepting guests.

X Bar Ranch: The Present

Some guests enjoy the post-hole diggin' and backbreakin' labor. They actually pay to do this. "It became kinda the joke in the coffee shop," Stan Meador says. "'What do you have your tour doing this week?'"

But let's face it: Cowboyin' in the twenty-first century isn't for everyone, and the X Bar aims to please for guests who really don't want to watch Chris Meador turn a calf into a steer with a flick of his knife.

"Soft adventure is what a lot of people are looking for," Stan Meador says. "That fits our family."

Horseback rides are offered ($14-$25). All rides are guided, with a minimum of four riders and no more than six or seven. There are trails, mostly single track, for riding your mountain bike. Hiking, birding, stargazing (with only one town in the whole county, you can imagine light pollution isn't a problem), and wildlife viewing are among the options. Mountain biking is quite popular on the X Bar. In 1998 the ranch put on a race that drew 500 people over the weekend and 300 racers on a Sunday morning.

One popular pastime on hikes and rides is trying to find old Indian middens, which are basically, for want of a better definition, barbecue pits used by Indians as far back as 10,000 years ago.

You can also go for a dip, but don't expect a heated, Olympic-size pool. Nope, for the true Western experience, the X Bar's swimming facility is an old stock tank, with walls about three feet thick, at the ranch headquarters built in the 1920s.

"This is where my dad, uncle, and aunt learned how to swim and swam growing up," Stan Meador says, "and we did, too, for that matter."

Lodging is found at the bunkhouses at Buckhorn Lodge. These are six rooms with baths, basically a hunter's cabin (after all, that's what they were built for) or line shack. They get the job done, though, and are equipped with air conditioning and heating. The lodge has a full kitchen and a television. Food and booze can be brought in, cookware and utensils are provided, but clean up the mess, will ya? You'll find the slim makings for breakfast in the kitchen area.

If the bunkhouse scene is too rustic for your taste, two houses are available for rent, the Live Oak Lodge and Cabins and the Round House.

The Round House might be the most popular.

"Grandpa wanted to do some kind of guesthouse, a place to get away," Stan Meador says. "My grandmother saw a magazine with a photo of a round house, and she liked the idea."

An architect/friend drew up some plans, and construction began in 1967. The Round House was completed in 1969. "No one's ever lived in it," Stan Meador says. "It's always been a place for entertaining."

The house, which, naturally, is round, provides a hidden retreat, complete with kitchen, living room, outside grill, and a giant window spanning two stories that provides a wonderful view of the ranch. The decor may be more 1960s-1970s than "cowboy," but the setting is rich and warm.

The family-run X Bar Ranch can provide a real Western vacation, but work isn't created for guests here.

That could be said about any place on the X Bar. It isn't really a "dude" ranch, nor is it a "B&B." Yet it is completely Western. "We're a Western family," Stan Meador says.

And a stay at the X Bar Ranch is a unique Western experience.

Cowboy Savvy

Interested in wool? The Eldorado Woolen Mill weaves fabrics from West Texas-produced virgin wool and mohair. If the X Bar is shearing sheep, you can watch wool come off the sheep, be taken to the mill, and turned into a blanket or rug. The mill, located at 409 SW Main St., was founded in 1939, and some of the machines used date to the 1880s. The showroom is open 8 A.M. to 5 P.M. Monday through Saturday, and tours are offered.

X Bar Ranch at a Glance

Address: P.O. Box 696, 5 N. Divide, Eldorado, TX 76936

Phone: (888) 853-2688, (915) 853-2688

Fax: (915) 853-3131

E-mail: xbar@compuserve.com

Internet: www.XBarRanch.com

Location: 20 miles southwest of Eldorado off Farm Road 2129.

Accommodations: 6 rooms, 2 houses, 1 lodge. Can accommodate 30-35 people total, plus campsites available for tenters (RV hookups planned).

Dining: Continental breakfast. Kitchens available for guests.

Rates: Standard lodging $40-$70 per person. Deluxe lodging $60-$90 per person. Extra persons/children $20-$50 per person.

Credit cards: American Express, Discover, MasterCard, Visa.

Handicap access: No.

Smoking: No.

Pets: No.

Things to do: Horseback riding, ranch tours, nature trails, wildlife viewing area, stargazing, participation in ranch activities, mountain biking, swimming (in stock tank), horseshoe pitching.

Season: Open all year. Restricted during hunting season.

Y.O. Ranch

Mountain Home

Guide Jim Hanks drives the Chevy truck-turned-into-safari-Jeep over the rough terrain of the Y.O. Ranch while I bounce around in the back with cameras, notepad, and hat, thinking that somehow I have been transported through the *Twilight Zone* into an episode of *Mutual of Omaha's Wild Kingdom*. "As Jim wrestles the hostile ostrich called Dumb Ass, I sit back and watch from afar." Only it doesn't work this way.

"Do you mind opening the gate?" Jim asks.

So that's why he's driving.

The ostrich's name is Junior, but the Y.O. staffers call him "Dumb Ass." Wise as an owl he isn't, but he's definitely protective of his pasture. Hanks has told me, "You're fine as long as you're in the vehicle, but once you get out you're *his*."

Holding a can of feed, Jim backs up to the Chevy, luring Junior away from the gate. Finally he dumps the feed onto the ground and floors it. "He's never caught on to this yet," Jim tells me before I leap out to open the gate, thinking: There's always a first time.

But Junior—no need to call him by that mean nickname and get on his bad side—isn't interested in me, and the gate swings open, Jim pulls through, and I lock Junior inside, safe and sound and out of Africa.

OK, so this is actually the Texas Hill Country, but with some fifty-five species of exotic animals, including zebras, sika, oryx, and eland, the Y.O. has a safari feel. Giraffes have eaten foliage off the trees so high up, even the country looks like Africa, not South Texas.

But wild game is only one aspect of the Y.O. Ranch. This is game preserve, hunting lodge, working ranch, and dude ranch rolled into one. It's also one of the Lone Star State's most famous ranches, ranking right up there with the JA, King, and XIT historic spreads.

Y.O. Ranch: The Past

Born in Riquewihr, Alsace-Lorraine, France in 1838, Charles Armand Schreiner moved to San Antonio, Texas, with his parents in 1852. Two years later, he joined the Texas Rangers but resigned in 1857 after his mother died and soon went into the cattle business in Kerr County. He served in the Confederate army's Third Texas Infantry and returned to his ranch after the Civil War.

After founding the Charles Schreiner Company, a banking, ranching, and mohair enterprise in 1869, Schreiner drove more than 300,000 head of cattle to Kansas between 1870 and 1880. He also was elected captain of a home militia group formed to fight Indians in 1875.

In 1880 Schreiner bought the Taylor-Clements Ranch and kept the Y.O. brand. The ranch grew to some 550,000 acres. He passed control of the Y.O. to his son Walter in 1916. Charles Schreiner died in 1927, and the sprawling South Texas spread was divided eight ways. Walter kept the Y.O. brand and turned over his part of the ranch to his wife, Myrtle Barton Schreiner, and their only son, Charles II, in 1933.

Charlie III took over in 1951. Times, including the economy, were changing, and a drought would crush many Texas ranchers over the next decade. Charlie III envisioned bringing exotic wildlife to the ranch, yet he wasn't interested only in offering big-game hunters the chance to bag a trophy without the expense of a trip to Africa. He also longed to preserve endangered species. The first import was the blackbuck antelope in 1955. Others followed, including gnu, beisa, and Himalayan tahr.

Charlie IV and Walter started running the Y.O. in 1976, and these days the Schreiners, including Gus and Louie, operate the storied ranch and game preserve, providing animals for hunters, true, but also for major zoos.

Y.O. Ranch: The Present

Fifty-two windmills pump water across the 40,000-acre ranch, and that's important because the Y.O. Ranch has no surface water. Oh, arroyos may flood during those savage thunderstorms prone to this part of Texas, but water is scarce in South Texas and the windmills mean life.

Jim Hanks feeds a hungry longhorn at the famous Y.O. Ranch in the Hill Country.

167

Of course, the Y.O. is still a working ranch with a herd of 2,000 longhorns. "All of the cattle are worked on horseback," Jim Hanks points out. The ranch is one of the few Texas guest ranches that actually offers an annual cattle drive, held Memorial Day weekend, where you can pay to help push them dogies (or stay out of the way of working cowboys), eat cowboy grub cooked over open fires, and sleep under the stars. You can even bring your six-shooter along to look the part, but you can't load it.

There are guided trail rides for one to twenty people, and the ranch can even do rides for a hundred on special occasions. Unlike many dude ranches, the Y.O. doesn't make the rides single-file, nose-to-tail. Children six and up can ride by themselves, and riding lessons are available.

Peak family season is April and May, and September through mid-January for hunters. Speaking of hunters, only 20,000 acres are open for hunting. Want to go after wild turkeys? It's $450. A blackbuck antelope will run you $1,500, an aoudad sheep $2,000, and a Nubian ibex $7,500. The guide fee is $200, meals and lodging $95, and a $500 nonrefundable deposit per hunter is required.

But if you don't like hunting, don't worry about the fate of all of the animals. As Jim Hanks says while driving through a game pasture: "Look at the fear in their eyes. The deer on this end of the ranch don't even know they're venison. They haven't been hunted for more than thirty years on this end of the ranch."

For boys and girls ages 9 to 16, there's the Y.O. Ranch Cowboy camp, one-week sessions (at $750 per child) that include cattle drives, roundups and branding, roping, barrel racing and pole bending, swimming, firearms safety, and a high ropes course and climbing tower, not to mention plenty of horseback riding (riding helmets mandatory).

Guests spending the night are housed in huge 1880-era log cabins. Cabins include the Boone Cabin, once a stagecoach stop in Waring; the Crockett Cabin, built near Fredericksburg circa 1868-70; the Wells Fargo Cabin, with the traditional room and a loft; and the Sam Houston Cabin, a schoolhouse from Center Point built in 1852. The cabins were dismantled and moved to the ranch to be restored and modernized. Some newer cabins have also been built. They may look old on the outside, but inside they are spacious and cozy.

If that's a little too rustic for you, well the swimming pool is nearby and offers a view of one of the pastures full of foreign wildlife. And then there's the Y.O. Lodge, complete with pool table, television, and a well-stocked bar. The lodge is always open, and there's an open bar at night.

Lodging includes three meals daily, but the sign at the grill, located at the ranch office, says it all: "This kitchen is not a restaurant. You eat when I'm ready."

Don't raise a fuss. One thing I've learned talking to cowboys and ranchers is that you never get on a cook's bad side. At the Y.O., mouthing off might get you fed to Junior the Ostrich.

Probably not, though. The Y.O. specializes in Texas friendly. But when you run the risk of Junior's wrath, why take chances?

Cowboy Savvy

You don't just drive up to the Y.O. Ranch for a daily visit, so make reservations first. A giant locked gate is located about seven miles from ranch headquarters—the ranch has to keep all of those animals inside, remember—but a phone is nearby to call for the combination to the lock. Once you have the combination, open the gate, drive through, and don't forget to close the gate behind you and lock it.

Y.O. Ranch at a Glance

Address: Highway 41 West, Mountain Home, TX 78058
Phone: (830) 640-3222, (800) 967-2624
Fax: (830) 640-3227
E-mail: gus@yoranch.com
Internet. www.yoranch.com

Location: 100 miles west of San Antonio on State Highway 41.

Accommodations: 15 rooms.

Dining: 3 meals daily.

Rates: $95 per person, includes meals and open bar at night.

Credit cards: American Express, MasterCard, Visa.

Handicap access: Yes.

Smoking: Yes.

Pets: Yes.

Things to do: Gift shop on site. Swimming pool, horseback riding, hunting, cattle drives, ranch tours, photo safaris, hiking, hayrides, off-road bicycling.

Season: Open all year. Restricted during hunting season September through mid-January.

I See By Your Outfit...

A working cowboy once told me his grandpa's thoughts on the proper attire for a waddie: *As long as you got a good hat and a good pair of boots, the rest of your outfit can look like trash.*

Take boots, for instance. In the 1870s and '80s during the heyday of the trail drives from Texas to Kansas and points north, a cowboy was likely to spend between $3 and $20 on a pair of boots. T.C. McInerney hung his shingle in Abilene, Kansas, in 1868. Charles H. Hyer began making high-heeled boots—with right and left lathes, too, by golly—along about 1875. And a gent named Joe Justin established what might be the forerunner of custom mail order in Spanish Fort, Texas, in 1879. Cowboys heading to Kansas would stop by his place near the Chisholm Trail to get measured, and Joe would have their boots ready on their return trip.

Now $20 might not seem like a wallet-buster today, but consider cowboys were drawing about a dollar a day then. Imagine their faces if they tried on the Ultimate Boot from Ammons Boots today. "$3,595?! You 'pect me to shovel hoss apples in them?"

Hats were often bought with open crowns and flat brims. One theory is the Montana Peak crown (think Mounties) was formed by picking up the hat with mittens (think cold in winter in Montana). Legend has it that J.B. Stetson created the cowboy hat by accident. He fashioned a hat from beaver and rabbit skins and formed it so it could fend off the heat and rain. Somebody saw the hat, liked it, paid Stetson five bucks, and J.B. was in business.

Stetson's famous "Boss of the Plains" had a low, open crown and flat brim. Before *Lonesome Dove*, a lot of people called one particular crown the Tom Horn, because the gunman was photographed in such a hat. After the hit miniseries, the crown became known as the Gus.

Cowboy hats cost from $1 to $5. A cap would run from fifteen to seventy cents. You could pick up a straw hat for two bits. Today's hat prices vary depending on quality, but you should expect to spend about $175 on a good custom-made rabbit-beaver blend, and on up to, say, $750 for a pure beaver hat. (You'd actually wear that in the rain?) Like boots, hats off the rack are a lot cheaper, but well-made custom jobs are worth the extra cash.

Oh, and two words about clothes. Real Texas cowboys in the 1880s wouldn't be caught dead in a pair of blue jeans. Levis were worn by sodbusters and miners, people who worked with dirt, and cowboys could be a mite snobbish about those kinds of things. They wore trousers made of wool, canvas, or cotton drill, sometimes reinforced with leather or canvas to protect their backsides and thighs. Of course, today's cowboy isn't ashamed to be seen in denim. And finally, the correct pronunciation for chaps is SHAPS. CHAPS are folks from England.

Ready to shop? Here are some suggestions:

General Mercantile

Big Bend Saddlery, P.O. Box 38, East Highway 90, Alpine, TX 79831. Phone: (800) 634-4502. Fax: (915) 837-7278. Hats, saddles, tack, spurs, rain slickers, and ropes—you can tell this place caters to the working cowboys in the area. But there is also a good selection of books along with plenty of other cowboy gift ideas. Big Bend Saddlery has been serving cowboys and cowboy wannabes since 1905.

Double D Ranch, 115 E. Main St., Fredericksburg, TX 78624. Phone: (877) 990-4959, (830) 990-4959. Fax: (830) 990-2440. This 4,000-square-foot store in one of Texas's most popular tourist towns opened in 1999. The Yoakum, Texas-based Double D Ranch specializes in women's fine clothing, home accessories, and bedding, all of which can be found at this store. Check out the bandana, Navajo, and cross pillows, and the company's home line, including beds and other furniture with a distinctive cowgirl attitude. Double D started out making clothes, and its line—from vests and jackets in suede, leather, and other fabrics, to skirts that would make Dale Evans proud—remain high quality and high fashion.

King Ranch Saddle Shop, 201 E. Kleberg Ave., P.O. Box 1594, Kingsville, TX 78364-1594. Phone: (800) 282-KING. Fax: (361) 595-1594. With a tradition that dates to 1867 when cattle baron Captain Richard King began hiring master saddlemakers, King Ranch Saddle Shop continues to pride itself on quality merchandise (and, yes, you can still find a saddle). The store is located in the 15,500-square-foot, two-story brick building in Kingsville's historic district that once housed the John B. Ragland Mercantile Company. The 1909 building, on the corner of Sixth Street and Kleberg Avenue, is on the National Register of Historic Places. Once known for high-end luggage, King

Ranch Saddle Shop now also offers a variety of men's and women's apparel, outdoor gear, books, and even home furnishings. Closed Sundays.

Luskey's/Ryon's Western Stores Inc., 2601 N. Main St., Fort Worth, TX 76106-7188. Phone: (800) 725-7966. (817) 625-2391. Fax: (817) 625-0457. For more than eighty years, Luskey's has been providing quality cowboy gear. You'll find everything from quality Carhartt outerwear to jeans and jewelry, boots to hats, plus custom bits and saddles.

Maverick Fine Western Wear and Saloon, 100 E. Exchange Ave., Fort Worth, TX 76106. Phone: (800) 282-1315, (817) 626-1129. Fax: (817) 626-1170. Located in the historic Stockyards district, Maverick offers gifts, jewelry, books, and apparel, with a wide selection of boots (including J.B. Hill) and hats (from premier hatmaker Rand's of Billings, Montana).

Maida's Belts & Buckles, 5642 Westheimer, Houston, TX 77056. Phone: (800) 785-6036, (713) 629-9091. Fax: (713) 629-9057. Maida's produces custom belts and wallets using alligator, crocodile, ostrich, lizard, and French calf leather. Of course, you need a pretty good buckle to go with such a belt, but don't worry. Maida's also manufactures sterling silver and 14K gold buckle sets. To top it off, the company carries several brand-name jewelry and buckle makers, including Bohlin Silversmith, Comstock Heritage, Douglas Magnus/Heartline, and Vogt Western, not to mention some vintage spurs and buckle sets.

M.L. Leddy's, 2455 N. Main St., Fort Worth, TX 76106. Phone: (817) 624-3149; 2200 W. Beauregard Ave., San Angelo, TX 76901. Phone: (915) 942-7655. M.L. Leddy opened shop in San Angelo in 1936 and expanded to Fort Worth in the 1940s. Originally a boots and saddle shop, Leddy's is now a high-end retailer where all customers, from movie stars to window shoppers, are treated like old friends. You'll find tack and hats (including a $750 model) and cowboy duds, and, yes, you can still get a pair of custom boots (starting at about $400) and a custom saddle (from around $1,400 on up).

Parts Unknown, 146 E. Main St., Fredericksburg, TX 78624. Phone: (830) 997-2055. This 2,000-square-foot store opened in 2000, joining other Parts Unknown outfits in Scottsdale, Arizona; Carmel, California; and Santa Fe, New Mexico. The store is part of Scully, which has been producing quality leather goods and apparel since 1906. Parts Unknown can outfit men and women no matter if your taste is North Country, Southwest, or the South Pacific.

Stelzig of Texas, 3123 Post Oak Blvd., Houston, TX 77056. Phone: (800) 922-1870, (713) 629-7779. Since way back in 1870, Stelzig has been supplying Westerners with everything from quality duds to custom-made saddles. Antone Stelzig started out supplying the Army, and five generations later, the Houston store continues to provide quality apparel, accessories, and—naturally—saddles.

Texas Jack's, 117 N. Adams St., Fredericksburg, TX 78624. Phone: (800) TEX-JACK, (830) 997-3213. Here's the best place in Texas for wannabe cowboys who want to be authentic. Many members of the National Congress of Old West Shootists and Single Action Shooting Society get their wardrobe here. Texas Jack's can outfit you from a pair of Coffeyville-style boots on up, with old-timey pants, a bib-front shirt, and a frock coat, not to mention bandanas, hats, vests, suspenders (you might need 'em to keep your pants up), and plenty of ladies wear. Plus, if you want to pack some iron (don't forget the waiting period and other federal firearms restrictions), Texas Jack's offers plenty of Cimarron Firearms reproduction weapons, including shotguns, revolvers, and rifles.

Custom Boots

(Tip: Call first to make an appointment if you want to be measured for a custom pair of boots.)

Rodney Ammons Boots, 10870 Pellicano Drive, Suite 290, El Paso, TX 79935. Phone: (915) 845-0323. Fax: (915) 845-0323. Rodney Ammons is one of the premier bootmakers in the world. He has outfitted Burt Reynolds, Hulk Hogan, Clint Eastwood, and other celebrities. Prices run from about $400 to "infinity." It just depends on your imagination and the limit on your MasterCard.

J.B. Hill Boot Company, 335 N. Clark Drive, El Paso, TX 79905. Phone: (915) 599-1551. Fax: (915) 599-1661. A relative newcomer (the company was founded in 1996), J.B. Hill has quickly made a name for itself with quality looks and a first-rate

Boots, from left, by J.B. Hill, Rodney Ammons, and Stallion, hat by Catalena Hatters. If you want to play cowboy, you might as well dress the part.

showroom thanks to president James M. Hill and Ivan Holguin, vice president of production and design. The company outfitted *The Horse Whisperer* and even put a pair on Marlon Brando. Prices start at $500 and rise to $4,000.

Kimmel Boot Company, RR 1, Box 36, Comanche, TX 76442. Phone: (915) 356-3197. This small custom shop turns out between 475 and 500 pairs of boots, in a variety of leathers, each year with an average price of $550. Kimmel, in the boot business for about twenty years, may not be as well known as Justin or Tony Lama, but those in the know laud these boots. "I refer to Eddie Kimmel boots as the Bentley of boots," says Roy Flynn of Back at the Ranch, a top Western retail store in Santa Fe, New Mexico. "If he's not the best, he's pretty close to it."

Little's Boots, 110 Division, San Antonio, TX 78214. Phone: (210) 923-2221. Fax: (210) 923-6818. Dave Little is continuing a family business his grandfather started in 1915, and daughter Sharon will take over for Dave. The prices top the scale, starting at $800. "People can't understand why we charge so much more than our competitors," Dave says. "I say, well, if you want quality you have to have the best craftsmen, and to get the best craftsmen you have to pay them a good wage."

Rusty Franklin Boot Company, 3275 Arden Road, San Angelo, TX 76901. Phone: (915) 653-BOOT. Franklin learned the boot business from the ground up while his father worked for M.L. Leddy, Franklin's grandfather. Prices run from $500 on up, with inlays from $250 to $1,000. Pay in advance by check, credit card, or money order and shipping is free.

Rocketbuster Boots U.S.A., 115 S. Anthony, El Paso, TX 79901. Phone: (915) 541-1300. Fax: (915) 562-1116. If you want boots with an attitude, this is the outfit for you. Attitude, as in 1940s retro, as in Roy Rogers or hula girls, chili peppers, baseballs.... If you're conservative, don't call for an appointment.

Oprah Winfrey, Mel Gibson, and Sylvester Stallone have pulled on a pair of Rocketbusters. Prices range from $550 to $950.

Stallion Boot & Belt Company, 100 N. Cotton, El Paso, TX 79901. Phone: (915) 532-6268. Fax: (915) 533-0996. Nice guy Pedro Muñoz Jr., an El Paso native, started this high-end company in 1982. His customers include Brooke Shields, Madonna, and Larry Hagman. "There's art in bootmaking," Muñoz says. "It's functional art, good art." Stallion boots are considered among the best designed in the business. Pedro's kind of art starts at $500 and goes up to $5,000.

Texas Traditions, 2222 College, Austin, TX 78704. Phone: (512) 443-4447. Any fan of singer-songwriter Jerry Jeff Walker knows all about the late, great Charlie Dunn, and at Texas Traditions you'll find the legend and quality are carried on. Dunn started Texas Traditions in 1977 and retired in 1986 on his 88th birthday. Sadly, Charlie passed away in 1993, but his apprentices keep using Dunn's methods to make boots. You'll need an appointment for measurement, not to mention your checkbook, MasterCard, or Visa. Be patient, too. Delivery time for a pair of boots is twenty-one months. Prices start at $775. A full alligator pair (top and bottom) sells for $4,100. Extras such as mule ears, spur guards, inlays, and initials are, well, extra.

Custom Hats

Catalena Hatters, 203 N. Main, Bryan, TX 77803. Phone: (800) 976-7818, (409) 822-4423. For about twenty years, Catalena has been making and fixing hats for customers. Prices range from $125 for a 5X, $225 for 10X, to $350 for an all-beaver 20X. The company can make just about any size, color, or style.

And as far as fixing hats is concerned, Catalena offers a hat renovation service, including cleaning, washing, reblocking, and new leather and lining for $45.

The Hat Store, 5587 Richmond, Houston, TX 77056. Phone: (713) 780-2480. Fax: (713) 780-8043. Hatmaking runs in Gary A. Cohen's blood. His grandfather, Sam Silver, founded the American Hat Company in Houston in 1915. Cohen's Hat Store features a wide selection of name brands including Stetson, Resistol, Bailey, and, naturally, American. Postpaid prices run from $79.50 for a 100 percent wool "Maxi-Felt" to $259.50 for a 10X beaver. American straw hats are also available, from $43.25 children's sizes to a $233.50 "Para-Panama." The Hat Store also offers a variety of hatbands, which run from $28 to hand-braided horsehair with engraved sterling conchos for $1,995. That's not a mistake. That's almost two grand for a hatband. You can also choose an 18K or 14K gold, sterling silver, or combination hatband with gems including diamonds, emeralds, or rubies. Call for a quote.

Limpia Creek Hat Company, 1204 Main Street, P.O. Box 1204, Fort Davis, TX 79734. Phone: (915) 426-2130. Since starting out as an apprentice in the early 1990s, Skeeter Roubison has outfitted working cowboys, re-enactors, and even Hollywood for TV movies such as *Dead Man's Walk* and *Streets of Laredo*. Felt prices run from about $99 for 5X (100 percent rabbit) to $750 for 100X (100 percent beaver), but the most popular styles are 10X (half-beaver/half-rabbit) at $165 and 20X (85 percent beaver, 15 percent mink) at $300-$350.

Peters Bros. Hats, 909 Houston Street, Fort Worth, TX 76102. Phone: (817) 335-1715. (800) TXS-HATS. Fax: (817) 335-4908. This local tradition in downtown Cowtown dates to 1911. Joe Peters Sr. and Joe Peters Jr. sell Western hats as well as fedoras from Stetson to Borsalino, or they can put you in a custom job such as the Shady Oak model of Amon Carter fame or the

Texas Hat, a cowboy-fedora hybrid that is sturdy as well as sharp-looking. Presidents, from Wilson to Clinton, have donned hats from this company.

Texas Hatters, P.O. Box 100, 5003 Overpass Road, Buda, TX 78610. (512) 295-4287, (800) 421-4287. Fax: (512) 312-0036. For three generations, the Gammage family (founder Marvin E. Gammage Sr., son Manny, and now Manny's daughter Joella Gammage-Nolen) has been making quality headgear for presidents (Ronald Reagan, George Bush), singers (Bob Dylan, Stevie Ray Vaughan), and actors (the *Lonesome Dove* miniseries cast). Texas Hatters might be most famous for its Half-Breed, a top made of hemp or Panama straw and the bottom of 100 percent New Zealand hare fur or 100 percent beaver fur (starting at $220). Fur felt prices run from $185 to $485, and Texas Hatters also offers services such as renovation, reblocking, and recreasing.

Ridin' the Chuck Line

A cowboy between jobs in the late 1800s might find himself riding the chuck line, heading from outfit to outfit to get a free meal from generous ranchers. Of course, he wanted to earn his grub—but a man's gotta eat. One name you didn't want to be called back then was a "chuck-line rider" or "grub-line rider." Those lazy rapscallions preyed on Western hospitality, heading from outfit to outfit for free meals, staying until they wore out their welcome, and never having any intention of actually cowboying for a living.

Then there were the cooks, like Wishbone of *Rawhide* fame, Hop Sing of *Bonanza* fame, and Roscoe Lee Brown's wonderful character in the 1972 John Wayne movie *The Cowboys*. In nineteenth-century Texas, some cooks were stove-up cowboys who couldn't punch cattle anymore; some were hired simply because they could drive a wagon. Being a gourmet chef wasn't the top prerequisite back then. Sweating over a cast-iron Dutch oven trying to feed worn-out waddies, it's no wonder cooks sometimes were a bit cranky. Maybe that's why they often earned nicknames like belly cheater, biscuit roller, dough-puncher, grease burner, grub spoiler, old woman, pot walloper, and mess moll.

Cowboy tip No. 1: At today's B&Bs, hotels, ranches, and resorts, you'll probably be better off calling the cook *sir* or *ma'am*.

If you're traveling down the trail, and Texas trails can be loooooong, you'll probably get hungry between stops. Texas is full of steakhouses, barbecue joints, and other restaurants. You can get your plate filled with ranch style beans and a chicken-fried steak almost anywhere. You can also get some overpriced shoe-leather if you're not careful, cooked by belly cheaters I'm certain. On the other hand, I stopped in Kingsville once and asked if someone could recommend a prime steakhouse or place to get a good hamburger. This is Kingsville, home of King Ranch, only the largest ranch in the world with pastures holding some 65,000 head of cattle. I was politely referred to Burger King. Well, at least there were plenty of Tex-Mex eateries in town.

There are the pretty good steakhouse chains, like Texas Land and Cattle Company and the tourist-minded (and loud) Trail Dust, across the Lone Star State. And there are plenty of places where real waddies and waddie wannabes can hang their hats, order a meal, and keep their bellybuttons from rubbin' against their backbones.

Here are some suggestions:

Angelo's, 2533 White Settlement Road, Fort Worth, TX 76107. Phone: (817) 332-0357. Lunch, dinner. This Cowtown icon serves schooners of ice-cold beer and tasty barbecue. The ribs are the best I've had, and this is coming from a South Carolina farm boy who thought for twenty-two years that barbecue was always made of pork. Angelo's is popular with tourists and locals alike, but remember to bring cash. The restaurant doesn't accept credit cards.

The Big Texan, 7701 E. Interstate 40, Amarillo, TX 79118. Phone: (806) 372-6000, (800) 567-7177. Lunch, dinner. Okay, it's total Texas cheese, from the mounted heads (game, not bad

Texas is full of fine places for cowboys and cowgirls to fill their bellies, including the famous Big Texan in Amarillo.

customers) on the walls to the waitresses in cowboy hats and badges, but you can get a great steak here, and the stuffed jalapeños ain't bad either. A video arcade, opry hall, and gift store are on site, and next door is the Big Texan motel. Steaks range from the $12.95 7.2-ounce Crockett-cut sirloin to the $27.95 22-ounce Trail Boss T-Bone. Or you can take a gamble on the 72-ouncer, $50 today compared to $9.95 in 1959. Eat it, along with the salad, shrimp cocktail, and baked potato, in an hour, and it's free. My waitress told me about one in eight who try it actually succeed. "More than you'd think," she said. Pork ribs, chicken, and shrimp are also offered, and there's a four-drink limit on liquor. Senior and kids menus are available, and a free cowboy hat comes with all kids meals. Bob Lee opened The Big Texan in 1959. The restaurant moved to its present location in 1970.

Bob's Steak and Chop House, 4300 Lemmon Ave., Dallas, TX 75219. Phone: (214) 528-9446. Dinner. Closed Sunday. Simply put, it's the best steak you'll find in Dallas, and there's some tough competition in Big D. Entrees are served with potato and a big carrot that Bugs Bunny would back-shoot a body for. You had best make reservations, then sit back and enjoy a hearty, well-cooked steak. While you're eating, check out the other patrons. Bob's is a great place to spot Dallas's movers and shakers. Pricey, but worth it.

Cattlemen's Steak House, 2458 N. Main St., Fort Worth, TX 76106. Phone: (817) 624-3945. Fax: (817) 624-1316. Lunch, dinner. A Cowtown icon since 1947, this restaurant in the historic Stockyards bills itself as the place "where real cowboys eat." Corn-fed beef, jumbo shrimp, and chicken are among the offerings. Entrees come with a baked potato or French fries and salad, with prices running from about $10 to $30 for supper and $6 to $11 for lunch. Heck, they'll even air-mail you some steaks ($75.95-$209.75) to cook yourself.

Centerpoint Station, 3946 S. Interstate 35, San Marcos. TX 78666. Phone: (512) 392-1103. Lunch, dinner. An antique store and soda shop combined, just across Interstate 35 from the San Marcos outlet stores, this is the perfect place for an old-fashioned burger and milk shake or malt. "We're just full of surprises," a friendly waitress says as she hands me a piece of homemade fudge on the house (and, no, I didn't tell her I was a travel writer). You can find old signs—check out the old Mobil horse on the roof—and the typical tourist fare (shot glasses, postcards, etc.) for sale while waiting for your order. The burgers are huge and worth the wait, and you can't top a rich vanilla shake. Keep in mind that because this is also an antique store, children should be accompanied by adults. Also note that Centerpoint Station closes at 6:45 P.M. Monday through Thursday, 7:45 P.M. Friday and Saturday, and 5:45 P.M. Sunday.

Cooper's Old Time Pit Bar-B-Que, 604 W. Young (Texas Highway 29), Llano, TX 78643. Phone: (915) 247-5713. Lunch, dinner. A longtime favorite considered one of the best barbecue joints in Texas, Cooper's sells barbecue by the pound. You can pick out your own piece of brisket—or pork chop, sirloin, ribs (beef and pork), sausage, chicken, even goat ribs and shoulder. Bread, beans, onion, jalapeños, and barbecue sauce are included with each order. So you choose a mouth-watering hunk of meat, and they'll cut it up for you. If you have room after pigging out, there's peach, blackberry, and apple cobbler available. If you can't get enough of Cooper's barbecue, call (877) 533-5553 to order by mail or request a catalog.

Country Inn, North Highway 36, Somerville, TX 77879. Phone: (409) 596-1222. Lunch, dinner. Closed Monday. The sign says, "We specialize in beef." Steaks are cut daily on site at this Somerville establishment that consistently looks as if it's filled with former, future, and current football players from Texas A&M University. Expect no-frills beef, a rib eye between 1 and 1¼ pounds, with salad, Texas toast, and fries or a baked potato. Steaks range from around $10 to $21, and burgers, seafood, and sandwiches are also offered.

The 1879 Townhouse Restaurant and Bakery, 111 S. College, Waxahachie, TX 75165. Phone: (972) 938-8971. Breakfast, lunch, dinner. Located in a circa 1890 building across from the courthouse, this family-style diner is popular with locals and tourists, including film crews when movies are being shot on location. An upstairs room can hold up to 80 people for rehearsal dinners, meetings, and parties. Breakfast runs from about $4 to $9, while burgers are in the $4.50 range and dinners include chicken-fried steak ($5.95 regular, $7.75 "Texas-sized") and mouth-watering roast beef ($5.75 half-order, $6.75 regular). A senior's menu is also available.

Friedhelm's Bavarian Inn, 905 W. Main, Fredericksburg, TX 78624. Phone: (830) 997-6300. Fax: (830) 997-6302. Lunch, dinner. Closed Monday. Okay, maybe German food isn't a real cowboy staple, but Texas and cowboys remain extremely popular in Germany. If you don't believe me, check out the number of European visitors at Texas guest ranches each year. Besides, Friedhelm's has a bar straight out of a *Bat Masterson* episode, and the food will certainly fill a cowboy or cowgirl. I'm a fan of the bratwurst, served with red cabbage, sauerkraut, and pan-fried potatoes or, my favorite, spatzle, all for only $7.95. Other favorites include the rump steak, a center-cut rib eye broiled in butter and garlic and topped with sautéed onions ($24.95). You'll find a lot of schnitzels, a good wine list, and "beers from the barrel." Friedhelm and Hilda Bopp opened this Fredericksburg highlight in 1980, and it's going strong.

The Iron Works Barbecue, 100 Red River, Austin, TX 78701. Phone: (512) 478-4855, (800) 669-3602. Fax: (512) 478-2272. Lunch, dinner. Housed in—yes, an old blacksmith shop—the old Weigl Iron Works building that is a state historical site, this Austin (and LBJ) favorite has been serving brisket and the like since the iron works business closed up shop in 1977 and was converted into a barbecue restaurant the following year. Branded boards cover the front of the building, part of the building's lore when customers would test Weigl-made branding irons. Jack Benny and Lucille Ball had brands made. Barbecue plates run from $5.40 to $11.05, while sandwiches are also reasonable ($2-$4). You can also order your own barbecue, seasonings, beans, and chili shipped via Federal Express.

Lost Maples Café, Highway 187, Utopia, TX 78884. Phone: (830) 966-2221. Breakfast, lunch, dinner. This small diner offers hearty meals at reasonable prices and the typical Texas-friendly waitresses. A chicken-fried steak runs from $5.50 to $6.95, and burgers and sandwiches range from under two bucks to no more than four. Breakfast, featuring omelets and breakfast tacos, is served from 7 to 11 A.M. Check out the pies if you have a sweet tooth: $2 a slice or, if you're a glutton, $10 for the whole thing.

Meyer's Elgin Smokehouse Bar-B-Que and Retail Outlet, 188 Highway 290, Elgin, TX 78621. Phone: (512) 281-3331. Lunch, dinner. The label on the barbecue sauce you find on the tables has this warning: "This is a very hot red pepper vinegar sauce. It is NOT for the faint of heart, so enjoy at your own risk." You can order smoked turkey breast, smoked pork ribs, pork garlic sausage, smoked beef brisket, and beef sausage by the pound. Sandwiches run from 99 cents for a pork garlic sausage wrap to $2.85 for a sliced beef sandwich. And, of course, the BBQ shack staples—pinto beans, potato salad, and coleslaw—are offered. So is the sauce, sold in 19-ounce bottles for $2.25—at your own risk, naturally.

Miss Hattie's Café and Saloon, 26 W. Concho Ave., San Angelo, TX 76903. Phone: (915) 655-6791. Lunch, dinner. Closed Sunday. Housed in the restored 1880s San Angelo National Bank, Miss Hattie's features the original tin ceiling, hospitality, and a full-service bar that is open until 2 A.M. After all, the original Miss Hattie was in the hospitality business; the bordello was in operation from the mid-1880s until Texas Rangers shut down the joint in 1946. Today the restaurant features everything from the Miss Hattie (lemon dill salmon, $15.95) and Brothel Burger (meat on a kaiser roll or sesame bun, $5.50) to the Mushroom and Onion Bourbon Steak ($20.95) and crab cakes served with cranberry sauce ($4.50).

The Reata, Bank One Building, 35th Floor, 500 Throckmorton St., Fort Worth, TX 76102. Phone: (817) 336-1009. Lunch, dinner. 203 N. Highway 118, Alpine, TX 79830. Phone: (915) 837-9232. Lunch, dinner. Closed Sunday. Al Micallef, Grady Spears, and Mike Evans founded The Reata restaurant in Alpine in 1995 (the Fort Worth location opened fourteen months later), naming it after the ranch from the 1956 epic motion picture *Giant*. Both locations feature cowboy atmosphere from Remington sculptures to cowhide chairs, and the food is definitely cowboy. After all, executive chef Grady Spears worked for a cattle company and was manager of Marathon's Gage Hotel. Meals come with sourdough bread (made from the oldest sourdough starter in the Southwest). Don't miss the jalapeño and cilantro soup ($3.95 cup, $4.95 bowl). The chicken-fried steak ($9.95 lunch, $12.95 dinner) and oven-roasted chicken ($8.95 lunch, $13.95 dinner) are always winners. Steaks begin at about $26. Come hungry because the portions are huge.

Stagecoach Inn, 1 Main, Salado, TX 76571. Phone: (254) 947-5111. Lunch, dinner. This historic Texas inn just off Interstate 35 between Dallas and Austin opened in the 1860s as the Shady Villa Hotel (it still operates as an inn, too). Its guests have included cattle kings Charles Goodnight and Shanghai Pierce as well as Sam Houston, who gave a speech against secession from the balcony, and George Custer, who was stationed temporarily in Texas after the Civil War. Place mats give a history of the inn.

The menu varies, but meals come with your choice of iced tea (heavy on the ice) or coffee, a salad, and dessert. Lunch offerings ranged from $7.95 to $12.95. A chicken-fried steak came complete with new potatoes, green beans, plenty of bread, and a wonderful banana fritter, plus peach cobbler for dessert. Not bad for ten bucks. Lunch is served from 11 A.M. to 4 P.M., and dinner from 5-9 P.M.

Y.O. Ranch, 702 Ross Ave., Dallas, TX 75202. Phone: (214) 744-3287. Lunch, dinner. So tell me: Where else can you find an ostrich burger? Like its namesake ranch in Mountain Home in the Texas Hill Country, this West End restaurant has a reputation for wild game. Sure, you can find catfish, foot-long enchiladas, steaks, and burgers, but you can also order quail and frog legs. Entrees range from $10.95 to $23.95 and are served with a choice of mushroom soup, soup du jour, or a four-leaf salad, plus a side dish and homemade bread.

Top Hands

Rodney Ammons

Rodney Ammons Boots, El Paso

Rodney Ammons always seems to draw a crowd, and not only to check out his latest boot designs. Ammons, Vietnam veteran, Tennessee good ol' boy, Elvis wannabe, purveyor of corny jokes, and pecan pie philosopher, is a hoot.

Consider his views on fashion:

- "I hate to keep calling it a cowboy boot because you don't have to be a cowboy to wear them. They look great with an Armani suit, shirt, and a bola. I wear that, and I think I look great."
- "Boots are convenient. You can stick a lot of stuff in them: wallets, pictures of your girlfriend, a derringer. . . ."

Or consider the time actor Burt Reynolds asked him to make some boots for country singers Dolly Parton, Kathy Mattea, and Tanya Tucker. Ammons told each singer he needed a thigh measurement.

Rodney Ammons of Rodney Ammons Boots in El Paso is one of Texas's premier bootmakers.

Ammons picks up the tale: "Dolly's so sweet. She fell for it. She asked why, and I told her it was because of balance. She said, 'Oh, I know all about balance.' Kathy Mattea said, 'I don't think so,' but Tanya said, 'Bull—. You want to feel my thigh, just go ahead and do it.'"

Funny, Ammons never needed my thigh measurement when he put me in a pair of his boots.

All kidding aside, Ammons is known for quality workmanship. He started out making shoes in Tennessee before Sam Lucchese, no slouch in the bootmaking trade, lured him into the high-end boot business. Later, Ammons worked with another bootmaking legend, T.O. Stanley, before he went into business for himself. Ammons Boots was founded in 1984.

"You need good materials, good workmanship, and finishing to make a great pair of boots," Ammons says. "I look for styling, too. Some people don't. A lot of people can make a well-built boot but they don't have the finishing and styling to go with that. I've seen some boots that are built extremely well with great material, but they look like hell."

By the way, Ammons wasn't kidding about hiding derringers in boots. He once made a pair for one of evangelist Billy Graham's bodyguards. "They had a big cross inlay in the center on the front," he says, "and a pouch inside for his derringer."

Charles Hudson

Texas Jack's, Fredericksburg

Charles Hudson has been selling firearms for thirty years, but these days he's a purveyor of more than just shooting irons. At Texas Jack's, you'll find him dressed in full cowboy regalia (well, maybe that turquoise bracelet isn't really cowboy), and that's fitting—no pun intended—when you consider that this store can outfit the waddies and waddie-wannabes from boots on up to hats, not to mention handguns, shotguns, repeaters, and buffalo rifles.

Texas Jack's has helped outfit various movies, from *Lonesome Dove* to *Geronimo: An American Legend*, to *Back to the Future III*, to *Son of the Morning Star*. But the company's primary clients are cowboy-action shooters, folks who dress up like cowboys and shoot in timed competition at (not living) targets. The Single Action Shooting Society and the National Congress of Old West Shootists are national organizations promoting this sport.

Sport?

"It's the largest growing sport in the U.S. right now," Hudson says. "I think the appeal is that everybody grew up on the old Westerns, and now they're living their childhood all over again and getting to play the part."

Of course, it can be costly. Cowboy shooters need two handguns, a shotgun, and a rifle, all replicas or authentic weapons from the frontier. That'll probably set you back $1,500—at least. And then there's the cowboy garb. The average shirt at Texas Jack's runs $50.

"It's not a sport for the poor," Hudson says.

But Texas Jack's isn't just for movies and cowboy shootists. After all, Fredericksburg is a tourist town, and out-of-staters, even out-of-country folks drop in from time to time.

The biggest seller?

Charles Hudson can outfit you from boots on up to hats as well as firearms at Texas Jack's in Fredericksburg.

"The bib-front shirt, or cavalry shirt," Hudson says. "They see it and remember it from the John Wayne movies."

Besides, Western wear remains popular, and authentic cowboy garb can be stylish, comfortable, and durable.

"I wear them all the time," Hudson says.

Bounce McFerran
Prude Ranch, Fort Davis

He had an associate's degree in engineering and a pretty good job in Oklahoma. But after a divorce, Bounce McFerran hitched his horse trailer to his pickup, got his good cowdog, and shucked it all for, to his way of thinking, a better way of life.

Cowboying.

That really doesn't follow the advice his grandfather gave him that sent McFerran to college: "Cowboys ain't gonna be forever. You better learn something you can fall back on."

Born and raised on a ranch in southeastern Oklahoma, McFerran found work as a cowboy and even worked with the Bureau of Land Management's wild mustang and burro program in Oklahoma. In 1993 McFerran got a call from Prude Ranch inviting him to come down for a few days. After the visit, he loaded up and drove back to Oklahoma. A few days later he got another call from Fort Davis, Texas: "When are you gonna come down and start working for us?"

McFerran is easy to find at Prude Ranch. He looks like a cowboy, from the Wilson's boots to the Limpia Creek hat that shields his sunburned, thick-mustached face. He looks happy, too.

Sure, working on a dude ranch isn't always fun and games. Not everything follows a script. Take the time McFerran was leading a trail ride with guests who insisted on taking their cell phones

Prude Ranch in Fort Davis has the best cowboys, and Bounce McFerran is friendly and knowledgeable.

with them. Everything was fine until the phones began their automatic tests. Now, electronic noises such as cameras and the like usually don't scare horses. But these phones were a different story.

"I mean to tell you we had wrecks everywhere," he says.

He can laugh at it now. (My guess is that he probably laughed, at least to himself, then, too.)

His favorite part of the job isn't working with horses or cattle. It's working with children, be it on the challenge course during summer camps or at the stables. Even more pleasing is when he has the opportunity to work with the blind or children with Down syndrome.

"The first time I did it, I was kind of on the nervous side," McFerran says, "especially with the Down syndrome children. But they pay attention and learn quite well. And they just light up. It's a great feeling to see that."

Cindi Meehan

The Nutt House Hotel, Elizabeth Crockett B&B, Granbury

While driving around the town square in Granbury for the first time, Cindi Meehan remarked that people could walk around here in nineteenth-century clothing and nobody would notice them because they would fit right in with the surroundings. Fast-forward some twenty years and it's this Connecticut native who is dressed like a pioneer woman in Granbury.

People notice her, of course, especially when she's passing out information about The Nutt House Hotel and Elizabeth Crockett B&B, both of which she manages. But she definitely fits in.

Cindi Meehan likes to dress the part as hostess at Granbury's Nutt House Hotel and Elizabeth Crockett B&B.

Meehan had worked in hotels in California before returning to Granbury. She met the owner of The Nutt House Hotel, and he soon asked her if she would like to manage the place.

"The very first time I set foot in the building, I was the manager," she says. "I never went in there. I thought they sold nuts there."

She works hard to promote the hotel and bed and breakfast. That's because this is more than a hobby. The businesses determine her income, and she's a single mother with a family to support. She started at The Nutt House in 1998, then landed a similar deal with the Elizabeth Crockett B&B in 1999. Running one hotel or B&B is usually a job for at least two, but it's the other way around for Meehan.

She's up in the morning, getting the continental breakfast ready for hotel customers and cooking up a delightful meal for B&B guests. She joked once that when a working cowboy took a room at The Nutt House, she told him that the first person up makes the coffee, never thinking for a moment that he'd beat her.

"Sure as shooting," she says, "I'm up at 5 A.M. and the pot's already brewing and he's sitting there already on his second cup of coffee."

On weekends, Meehan usually dresses in pioneer costumes. Her cell phone—"six-shooter," she calls it—is strapped on an ankle. "I don't know how pioneer women survived the summers in these outfits," she says. You try doing laundry in the worst Texas summer in heavy clothing.

No complaints, though, despite the heavy workload. This is her niche.

"Twenty years ago, I should have been doing this," she says. "I didn't know it then, but I was being prepared for this."

Skeeter Roubison

Limpia Creek Hat Company, Fort Davis

Skeeter Roubison started work here out of boredom as much as anything. He ran a bar at night and was looking for a day job. Someone suggested he check in at the hat company that was opening up, so he dropped in and landed a job. He started out building hat racks and doing other carpentry chores before the store opened in 1993, and then the boss suggested he "go make a hat." Roubison apprenticed for three months.

Today, he pretty much runs Limpia Creek Hat Company, from taking measurements and orders to shaping and finishing the hats and shipping them out. He also sweeps out the joint.

A native Texan born in Andrews and raised in Eldorado, Roubison attended Sul Ross State University in Alpine as an art major. Well, there's some art in making a cowboy hat.

"Oh, I don't know about that," he says. "You have to have an eye to know where to start."

At Limpia Creek, Roubison finds himself making a wide variety of hats (75 percent are mail order). Hats for working cowboys in the area. Maybe a green hat for Saint Patrick's Day. Historical hats for cowboy and mountain-man re-enactors. Top hats. Bowlers. Railroad hats. Even hats for movies: including forty-two for *Dead Man's Walk*, one for *Streets of Laredo*, and helping outfit *Dancer, Texas*. If folks come in wanting that John Wayne or Buffalo Bill Cody hat, Roubison has plenty of photos from movies and history books to help the customer pick the right hat.

He takes pride in the 1883 army regulation hat he made. Roubison got the measurements from the Smithsonian Institution and went to work. "It's different," he says of making historically accurate hats. "It takes a lot of detail and time to make sure it's right." When he was finished, his hat's weight was only nine-hundredths of an ounce off the original.

Skeeter Roubison can put a quality lid on anyone who visits Limpia Creek Hat Company in Fort Davis.

Roubison churns out between 600 and 1,000 hats a year. He would like to get those numbers up to about 3,000. Of course, that's kind of hard when you're basically a one-man show in a town as small as Fort Davis.

"Yeah," he says, "we do it all. This is a drop-off for dry cleaning. I do light tack and repair to janitor to carpentry work here."

Author's Note

This book is a guide. Keep in mind that restaurants, stores, manufacturers, B&Bs, hotels, ranches, and resorts are businesses, and businesses change ownership, change policies, have staff turnover, go out of business. At least four places I visited while researching this book were on the market. Two places I contacted during the preliminary research for this book went out of the hospitality business. One restaurant I thought about including was closing its doors. Websites change, and so do phone numbers. Like the actor in the commercial says about area codes: There's too many of 'em and they keep a-changin'.

Two places I visited and had intended on including in this book didn't cut the mustard. I found the staffs in need of a crash course in Texas friendly, which reminded me of what one hospitable host told me: "You can have the best rooms and food in the world, but if the customer service isn't there, then your guests aren't coming back, nor should they."

On the other hand, there are probably several gems waiting to be discovered. Texas is filled with historic accommodations, wonderful B&Bs, beautiful hotels, and exotic ranches and resorts.

Check things out before you go. Get information from local chambers of commerce and tourism bureaus. Don't forget: This is your vacation.

Happy trails!

Johnny D. Boggs
Santa Fe, New Mexico

Appendix A

Recommended Readin' and Viewin'

Of course, if you truly want to get in the Texas cowboy mood before your trip, here are a few suggestions (in no particular order).

Novels to Read

The Time It Never Rained (1973). San Angelo's Elmer Kelton examines the brutal West Texas drought of the 1950s. Rancher Charlie Flagg—Kelton's greatest character, and he's known for his great characterizations—faces changing times and attitudes and unchanging weather. Of course, you can't go wrong with any Kelton novel.

My Pardner (1963). Texas-born Max Evans takes a Mark Twain-ish approach in this lighthearted look at a Depression-era horse drive from Starvation, Texas, to Guyman, Oklahoma. Evans based this short novel, which can be found in *Hi Lo to Hollywood: A Max Evans Reader,* on an actual horse drive he made when he was ten years old.

Not Between Brothers (1996). Well, heck, you have to have an Alamo book or something dealing with the Texas revolution, and David Marion Wilkinson's long but lyrical look at a white man, Remy Fuqua, and a Comanche, Kills White Bear, is one of the best historical novels about early Texas. This one covers the period from 1816 to 1861.

Lonesome Dove (1985). It's mandatory in Texas to include this Larry McMurtry epic. After all, it won a Pulitzer as well as a Spur Award from the Western Writers of America, and was turned into an excellent miniseries starring Robert Duvall and Tommy Lee Jones. In case you've been on Mars for the past twenty-five years, the plot follows two former Texas Rangers on a cattle drive from South Texas to Montana in the 1870s. It's a great book, too.

The Trail to Ogallala (1964). *Lonesome Dove* notwithstanding, Benjamin Capps's novel is probably the most authentic look at a cattle drive since Andy Adams's *Log of a Cowboy* way back in 1903. These waddies, as realistic as you'll find in any novel this side of Elmer Kelton country, drive a herd of longhorns from Texas to Ogallala, Nebraska. It also won a Spur.

Nonfiction Books to Read

The Chisholm Trail (1954). Wayne Gard corrects the myths about the most famous of the cattle trails and shows what working cowboys had to face on the often boring but sometimes dangerous journey from Texas to Kansas. The actual Chisholm Trail, by the way, led from the Red River in present-day Oklahoma to Wichita, Kansas, but it has become synonymous with Texas.

Cowboy Culture (1981). Historian David Dary traces the cowboy lifestyle from its beginnings to its place in mythology, a span of five centuries. He looks at the Spanish influence, the trail drives, the open range, the cowtowns, and the end of the era, even the equipment.

The Longhorns (1941). Any serious student of Texas knows you start and end with J. Frank Dobie. *The Longhorns* is an intelligent, witty, and entertaining read that examines the history, characteristics, and "outlaws" of the most recognizable of all bovines.

Lone Star: A History of Texas and the Texans (1968). Native Texan T.R. Fehrenbach chronicles the Lone Star State from prehistoric times to the early explorers to the Mexican rule and the war for Texas independence to the days of the Republic of Texas to the Civil War to the Indian wars to the Kennedy assassination and on up. In short, here's everything you need to know about Texas.

The Last Comanche Chief: The Life and Times of Quanah Parker (1995). There is more to Texas than cowboys. Quanah was the most famous Comanche by far, the son of a Comanche chief and Cynthia Ann Parker, who was taken during a raid on Parker's Fort near present-day Mexia in 1836. Quanah led his people in a bloody war against white encroachment, then led them in the even more difficult journey on "the white man's road." There are many excellent biographies of Quanah, but this one by Bill Neeley is the best documented and most insightful.

CDs to Hear

Thank Heavens for Dale Evans (1990). Before they became internationally famous and across the radio and music video airwaves everywhere you turn, the Dixie Chicks were a four-gal group that blended Robin Lynn Macy's Texas twang, Laura Lynch's beautiful voice, and sisters Martie and Emily Erwin's excellent fiddle-viola-banjo-playing.

Culture Swing (1992). The warm vocals of Tish Hinojosa showcase a blend of Tex-Mex, Hispanic, and cowboy music. You don't even have to understand the language to recognize the beauty of her Spanish songs, while "In the Real West" makes you think of cowboys, dance halls, and Saturday night.

My Rifle, My Pony and Me (1993). If this Bear Family German import can't get you in the cowboy mood, nothing can. It includes the title track by Ricky Nelson and Dean Martin (from the John Wayne movie *Rio Bravo*), to the great Western movie and TV themes "Gunfight at O.K. Corral" (Frankie Lane), "High Noon" (Tex Ritter), "Ballad of Davy Crockett" (Fess Parker), and "Rawhide" (Frankie Lane again). There's even Lorne Greene singing the "Bonanza" theme.

Ride the River (1994). There ought to be a law against Mike Blakely. The Marble Falls gent not only can write great novels (*Shortgrass Song, Comanche Dawn*), he's also a brilliant cowboy singer/songwriter who can pick one mean mandolin. He even looks like an 1880s Texas cowboy, the jerk. *Ride the River* features plenty of original cowboy tunes, including the title track.

Tribute to the Music of Bob Wills and the Texas Playboys (1993). The Ray Benson-led Asleep at the Wheel pays homage to the King of Western Swing, and gets help from George Strait, Lyle Lovett, Suzy Bogguss, Merle Haggard—who had a fine Wills offering himself with *A Tribute to the Best Damn Fiddle Player in the World (or, My Salute to Bob Wills)* in the early '70s—and others. Covered are "All Night Long," "Across the Alley from the Alamo," "Blues for Dixie," "Big Ball's in Cowtown," and other classics.

Movies to Watch

Red River (1948). Director Howard Hawks's first Western starred John Wayne as a tyrannical cattle baron and Montgomery Clift, in his first film, as the Duke's foster son. After the Civil War, they are forced to drive their herd of cattle to the railheads up north. Often compared to *Mutiny on the Bounty*, this epic, filmed in gritty black and white, features one of Wayne's best performances as a Captain Bligh out west.

The Good Old Boys (1995). Tommy Lee Jones directed, co-wrote, and starred in this made-for-cable adaptation of the Elmer Kelton novel. Jones plays Hewey Calloway, an itinerant cowboy facing the changing times in 1906 who visits his brother's Texas farm and becomes smitten by schoolmarm Sissy Spacek. Filmed on location in West Texas, including Fort Davis National Historic Site.

Winchester '73 (1950). James Stewart wins a one-in-a- thousand Winchester repeater in Dodge City, Kansas, then chases the rogues, led by Jimmy's evil brother (Stephen McNally), who have stolen his rifle across Kansas, the Indian Nations, past Doan's Store on the Red River, and to Tascosa, Texas. By the way, when Stewart rides after McNally for the final showdown, he gallops past some saguaro cacti, which you ain't gonna find in the Lone Star State, my friend.

Giant (1956). Rock Hudson, Elizabeth Taylor, and James Dean (who died in a car crash shortly before filming was complete) star in this adaptation of Edna Ferber's novel about a Texas cattle baron (Hudson), his stranger-in-a-strange-land wife (Taylor), and their family's trials and tribulations. Cheesy? You bet, but this must-see movie, highlighted by Dean's greatest performance, features wonderful location scenes (filmed around Marfa) and a strong script that pulls no punches when addressing prejudice.

The Searchers (1956). I mark this John Ford classic as the best movie ever made, but don't take my word for it. Martin Scorcese, George Lucas, Steven Spielberg, and a host of other filmmakers swear by it. John Wayne gives his best uncompromising performance ever as the hard-driven Ethan Edwards (the Duke named one of his sons Ethan), who spends years obsessed with finding his nieces kidnapped by Comanches. The Monument Valley location isn't Texas, but the characters sure are.

Appendix B

Selected Contacts

Amarillo Convention & Visitors Council, P.O. Drawer 9480, Amarillo, TX 79105. (800) 692-1338. (806) 374-1497.

Austin Convention & Visitors Bureau, 201 E. Second St., Austin, TX 78701. (800) 926-2282. (512) 478-0098.

Bandera County Convention & Visitors Bureau, P.O. Box 171, Bandera, TX 78003. (800) 364-3833. (830) 796-3045.

Bed & Breakfast Texas Style, 4224 W. Red Bird Lane, Dallas, TX 75237. (800) 899-4538. (972) 298-8586.

Big Bend Area Travel Association, P.O. Box 401, Alpine, TX 79831. (915) 837-2326.

Fort Davis Chamber of Commerce, Box 378, Fort Davis, TX 79734. (800) 524-3015.

Fort Worth Convention & Visitors Bureau, 415 Throckmorton, Fort Worth, TX 76102. (800) 433-5747. (817) 624-4741.

Historic & Hospitality Accommodations of Texas, P.O. Box 1399, Fredericksburg, TX 78624. (800) HAT-0368.

Texas Department of Economic Development, Tourism Division, P.O. Box 12728, Austin, TX 78711. (512) 462-9191.

Texas Hotel & Motel Association, 900 Congress Avenue, Suite 201, Austin, TX 78701. (512) 474-2996.

Texas Parks and Wildlife Department, 4200 Smith School Road, Austin, TX 78744. (800) 792-1112. (512) 389-4800.

San Angelo Convention & Visitors Bureau, 500 Rio Concho Drive, San Angelo, TX 76903. (800) 375-1206. (915) 653-3162.

Appendix C

Cowboy Glossary

If you want to speak the part of a cowboy, you need to know the language. Here's a sampling:

airin' the lungs: expressing displeasure with language not used in polite society.

dally: wrapping the rope around the saddle horn after a successful toss.

drag: the position, or rider(s), on a trail drive who push the slowest cattle and eat the most dust since they're at the tail end of the herd.

flank: the position, or rider(s), between swing and drag, about two-thirds of the way behind the point, on a trail drive.

hackamore: a halter for a horse.

maverick: an unbranded animal; also, a lighthearted TV series starring James Garner and Jack Kelly.

point: the position, or rider(s), at the head of the herd on a trail drive.

prairie oysters: uh-hum . . . beef testicles, fried or roasted. A King Ranch cowboy once told me while branding and castrating calves that prairie oysters are the best eating in the world. To which I replied: "I'll take your word for it."

quirt: a short riding whip.

remuda: the string of horses on a trail drive.

ride the river: the ultimate cowboy compliment. If a cowboy says you're one to ride the river with, your head has a right to swell.

sugan: bedroll

swing: the position, or rider(s), on a trail drive where the cattle begin to swell, about a third of the way behind the point.

tasting gravel: bucked off a horse. Also: dirtying your shirt, busted, piled, spilled, wrecked, rodeoed, dumped, dusted. . . .

waddies: cowboys.

wrangler: a horse herder.

Appendix D

Recipes: Food for Thought from the Pot Wallopers

FRIED BEEF TENDERLOIN,
The Hotel Limpia, Fort Davis

Ingredients: 2 pounds beef tenderloin, 1 cup flour, 1 teaspoon pepper, 1 teaspoon Lawry's seasoning salt, ½ teaspoon garlic powder, ½ cup milk, ½ cup butter or vegetable oil.

Instructions: Slice tenderloin into 6 thin pieces as if you were slicing thin fillets. Pound meat with a meat tenderizer until desired thickness. Melt butter in a frying pan over medium heat. Mix flour, pepper, salt, and garlic powder. Dip tenderloin slices into flour mixture and press flour into meat. Dip into milk. Dip into flour mixture again. Sauté until desired doneness. Remove from pan, drain on paper towel, and keep warm until all slices have been prepared. Serve with peppered cream gravy and a grilled jalapeño.

Serves: 6.

PUMPKIN PANCAKES AND PRALINE SAUCE,
Texas Stagecoach Inn, Vanderpool

Ingredients: 1 can canned pumpkin, 2 cups flour, 4 tablespoons sugar, dash of salt, 4 teaspoons baking powder, 2 cups milk, 2 eggs, 2 teaspoons cinnamon, 1 cup sour cream, 2 8-ounce packages of cream cheese, softened.

Directions: In a large bowl, combine all ingredients except cream cheese. Bake small pancakes on heated griddle until edges are brown and bubbles rise to the surface of the pancake; turn them over and bake until golden. Then pancakes will be very light. While they are still warm, spread the cream cheese over them and roll like a crepe. Serve with hot Praline Sauce.

Praline Sauce

Ingredients: 2 cups toasted walnuts, chopped; 2 sticks butter; dash of cinnamon; 3 cups of Karo syrup; ¾ cup dark brown sugar; 1 tablespoon vanilla; ¼ teaspoon maple flavoring.

Directions: Combine and heat to boiling on medium heat. Continue until thickened. Serve over pancakes.

Serves: 8-10.

GRILLED TEXAS BOBWHITE QUAIL WITH SHERRY-MAPLE GLAZE,
Rough Creek Lodge, Glen Rose

Ingredients for marinade: ½ cup vegetable oil, 2 teaspoons ground ancho chili, 1 teaspoon fresh chopped thyme, 1 teaspoon chopped fresh garlic, 1 teaspoon fresh ground black pepper, ½ teaspoon fresh ground cumin, 1 tablespoon sherry vinegar, 1 tablespoon kosher salt.

Directions: Mix all ingredients and pour over 6 bobwhite quail. Let marinate for at least two hours.

Glaze ingredients: ¾ cup sherry vinegar, ¾ cup pure maple syrup.

Directions: Place sherry vinegar and maple syrup in stainless steel pan and cook over low heat until it is reduced by half and thick like syrup.

To cook the quails: Remove from marinade and grill over hot coals for 8 to 10 minutes or until cooked all the way through. Place each quail on a warm plate and top with a little of the glaze. A nice accompaniment would be some soft stone ground grits.

Serves: 6.

Bibliography

Adams, Andy. *Log of a Cowboy*. New York: Leisure Books, 1976.

Adams, Ramon F. *Western Words: A Dictionary of the American West*. Norman: University of Oklahoma Press, 1968.

Baker, T. Lindsay. *Ghost Towns of Texas*. Norman: University of Oklahoma Press, 1986.

Banks, Suzy. "Hey, Dude." *Texas Monthly*, October 1999.

_____. "The Best of Small-Town Texas." *Texas Monthly*, March 1999.

Boggs, Johnny D. "Homes of the Cattle Barons." *True West*, March 2000.

Cibolo Creek Ranch, The. (no author listed). Houston: Southwestern Holdings, 1994.

Cummings, Joe. *Texas Handbook*, Fourth Edition. Chico, California: Moon Publications, 1998.

Dary, David. *Cowboy Culture*. New York: Avon Books, 1981.

Dobie, J. Frank. *The Longhorns*. Austin: University of Texas Press, 1990.

Dooley, Claude, and Dooley, Betty. *Why Stop? A Guide to Texas Historical Roadside Markers*, Second Edition. Houston: Lone Star Books, 1985.

Durham, Philip, and Jones, Everett L. *The Negro Cowboys*. Lincoln: University of Nebraska Press, 1965.

Fehrenbach, T.R. *Lone Star: A History of Texas and the Texans*. New York: American Legacy Press, 1983.

Forbis, William H. *The Cowboys*. Alexandria, Virginia: Time-Life Books, 1973.

Frazer, Robert W. *Forts of the West*. Norman: University of Oklahoma Press, 1965.

Gard, Wayne. *The Chisholm Trail*. Norman: University of Oklahoma Press, 1964.

Hamilton, Allen Lee. *Sentinel of the Southern Plains: Fort Richardson and the Northwest Texas Frontier 1866-1878*. Fort Worth: Texas Christian University Press, 1988.

Horton, Thomas F. *History of Jack County*. Jacksboro: Gazette Publishing, no date.

Hunter, J. Marvin. Editor. *The Trail Drivers of Texas*. Austin: University of Texas Press, 1992.

Knight, Oliver. *Fort Worth: Outpost on the Trinity*. Fort Worth: Texas Christian University Press, 1990.

Manns, William, and Flood, Elizabeth Clair. *Cowboys & The Trappings of the Old West*. Santa Fe: Zon International Publishing, 1997.

McCutcheon, Mark. *The Writer's Guide to Everyday Life in the 1800s*. Cincinnati: Writer's Digest Books, 1993.

Moss, Sue. *National Historic Register Application*, courtesy of Cibolo Creek Ranch.

Moulton, Candy. *The Writer's Guide to Everyday Life in the Wild West*. Cincinnati: Writer's Digest Books, 1999.

New Handbook of Texas Online, The. (Internet) http://www.tsha.utexas.edu/cgi-bin

Nored, Mildred Bloys, and Wiant, Jane. *Early Homes and Buildings of Fort Davis, Texas*. Fort Davis: Bloys Books, 1997.

O'Keefe, Eric. *West Texas and the Big Bend*. Houston: Gulf Publishing Company, 1995.

Scobee, Barry. *Fort Davis, Texas 1583-1960*. Fort Davis: Fort Davis Company, 1963.

_____. *Old Fort Davis*. Fort Davis: Bartholomew House, 1984.

Selcer, Richard F. *Hell's Half Acre*. Fort Worth: Texas Christian University Press, 1991.

Sizemore, Deborah Lightfoot. *The LH7 Ranch in Houston's Shadow: The E.H. Marks' Legacy From Longhorns to the Salt Grass Trail.* Denton: University of North Texas Press, 1991.

Spears, Grady, and Walsh, Robb. *A Cowboy in the Kitchen: Recipes from Reata and West of the Pecos.* Berkeley: Ten Speed Press, 1998.

Sutherland, Lin. "Texas' Hill Country Ranches." *Persimmon Hill,* Spring 1998.

Utley, Robert. *Fort Davis National Historic Site, Texas.* Washington: National Park Service, 1965.

Walters, Gwen Ashley. *The Great Ranch Cookbook: Spirited Recipes & Rhetoric from America's Best Guest Ranches.* Carefree, Arizona: Guest Ranch Link, 1998.

Worcester, Don. *The Chisholm Trail: High Road of the Cattle Kingdom.* Lincoln: University of Nebraska Press, 1980.

Index (By City)